PRIVACY

PRIVACY

Garret Keizer

BIG IDEAS // small books

PICADOR

New York

www.picadorusa.com
www.twitter.com/picadorusa ▪ www.facebook.com/picadorusa
www.picadorbookroom.tumblr.com

Picador® is a U.S. registered trademark and is used by
St. Martin's Press under license from Pan Books Limited.

For book club information, please visit www.facebook.com/
picadorbookclub or e-mail marketing@picadorusa.com.

Grateful acknowledgment is given for permission to quote from
the following poem: "The Place Where We Are Right," in
The Selected Poetry of Yehuda Amichai, edited and translated by
Chana Bloch and Stephen Mitchell. © 1996 by Chana Bloch
and Stephen Mitchell. Reprinted by permission of the
University of California Press.

Library of Congress Cataloging-in-Publication Data

Keizer, Garret.
    Privacy / Garret Keizer.—1st ed.
        p. cm.
    Includes bibliographical references.
    ISBN 978-0-312-55484-2 (paperback)
    ISBN 978-1-4668-0200-1 (e-book)
    1. Privacy. I. Title.
    BF637.P74.K448 2012
    302'.14—dc23

                        2012014919

First Edition: August 2012

10 9 8 7 6 5 4 3 2 1

For Kathy and Sarah

CONTENTS

18.
ANOTHER NATIVITY: *A Conclusion* 149

"Bastards!" Larry would exclaim when a blogger raised concerns about user privacy. "Bastards!" they would say about the press, the politicians, or the befuddled users who couldn't grasp the obvious superiority of the technology behind Google's products.

—Douglas Edwards, *I'm Feeling Lucky:*
The Confessions of Google Employee
Number 59

Now, gods, stand up for bastards!

—William Shakespeare, *King Lear*

PRIVACY

LET'S BEGIN BY DOING A LITTLE SHARING
A PREFACE

> Man did not enter into society to become *worse* than he
> was before, not to have fewer rights than he had before,
> but to have those rights better secured.
>
> —THOMAS PAINE, *COMMON SENSE*

Does anything say so much about the times we live in as the fact that the word *sharing* has almost everything to do with personal information and almost nothing to do with personal wealth?

Of course, some will answer that we live in times when information *is* wealth. Generally these are people who have good teeth and drive nice cars. When they sit down to eat, which they do regularly and well, you can bet they're not eating information.

To say the same thing in slightly different words: You and I belong to a society in which the gap between the rich and the poor is widening even as our personal privacy shrinks. It is the contention of this book that these two phenomena are connected, and connected in a number of ways.

To state just one of those ways: We tend to think of our right to privacy as a value that came about with the historical growth of the middle class. If, as current indices of income suggest, the middle class is vanishing, then it should come as no surprise if the privacy of all but a few people is vanishing with it.

This book also contends that privacy is important and worthy of preservation. It is important and worthy of preservation for the simple reason that human beings are important and worthy of preservation. These may seem like rather obvious statements, though if they were that obvious or universally believed we would not be so easily resigned to losing our privacy and to watching so many of our fellow human beings fall further and further behind in health, in education, in political power, and in privacy.

That privacy is a good thing for human beings is not hard to establish. Were it not a good thing, the wealthier among us would not enjoy more of it than the less wealthy do. The best things in life may be free, but that seldom prevents those at the top of the food chain from appropriating a lion's share of the best things. Air is free, but it tends to smell better in Malibu than in East L.A.

Some would contend that Americans, like citizens of other democratic nations, all have an equal right to privacy regardless of the air they breathe—and in some notable if not always typical instances, courts in the United States have agreed. But the right to privacy depends in large part on one's opportunities for enjoying a private life. Americans are all guaranteed freedom of the press, too, but what does that mean if you have never been taught to read or write?

In the hopes of giving as thorough an introduction as possible to the big idea of privacy, this small book will range over a number of topics, but it will always come back to the basic themes I've stated above: the sacredness of the human person and the value of privacy; the things we share and the things we don't; the ways we make ourselves lonely and the ways we mistake alienation for a private life.

I should add that giving a thorough introduction to privacy is not the same thing as giving it an airtight definition, a project I regard as both impossible and unwise. That's not to say I won't try for a tentative definition later in the book, or that I agree with a scholar who says, "Perhaps the most striking thing about privacy is that nobody seems to have any very clear idea what it is."

In fact, I think most of us do have a clear idea—if not clear enough to define the word, then clear enough to express the need behind it. Clear enough to say "Let me alone." Not to be confused with "Leave me alone," "Let me alone" is ever the cry of privately disposed women and men, of anyone who struggles to keep some reasonable hold on his or her short and not always sweet life. We are entitled to that cry.

That said, we will cry it in vain so long as we settle for anything less than a beloved community, with liberty and justice for all.

FRIENDS AND ENEMIES

AN INTRODUCTION

A friend is someone before . . . [whom] I can think aloud.
—RALPH WALDO EMERSON, "FRIENDSHIP"

I am writing in early November, about the time when I begin looking in my rural delivery mailbox for the annual Christmas letter that will come from my former college classmate Ralph. It is one of the longest and most welcome letters I receive during a year filled with robust correspondence. His letters of the past several years have been especially dear to me. Not only are they every bit as colorful as their antecedents of thirty years ago—full of his adventures surfing and hiking up and down the Pacific Coast, reading his poetry aloud at slams and soup kitchens, reuniting with old flames from his Springsteen days on the Jersey Shore—they're now infused with that sense of redemption that comes from a second chance. Not long ago I feared that my long friendship with Ralph might be at an end.

The trouble came when Ralph casually revealed to me that he had been scanning my paper letters and pasting the texts of his into a single electronic document that he e-mailed to his friends and associates. Presumably he was sharing our correspondence because he thought it valuable, and sharing the fact with me because he thought I'd be flattered. I wasn't. In fact, I was horrified at the thought of complete strangers reading what amounted to signed disclosures of family health problems, professional difficulties, spiritual doubts. Our custom over the years had been to confine our exchanges to a

single yearly letter, but I dispensed with custom and rang
him up after the holidays.

"What the hell are you doing, Ralph?" I demanded. I
should add that, in the interests of privacy, Ralph is not my
friend's real name. Nor is *hell* the word I used after "What
the."

The episode is likely to strike some readers as quaint in
its twenty-first-century context: two middle-aged men still
communicating by posted letter, one of them making only
minimal use of technology and the other offended in a way
that seems vaguely Victorian—to say nothing of a larger
circle of acquaintances who apparently have the patience to
read an entire correspondence by a pair of third parties, and
with no option of posting a comment or two of their own, to
click on "Like" or turn down a virtual thumb. What I considered an intolerable breach of privacy would strike others
as pretty innocuous, and even pretty private—especially when
compared to what happened to Tyler Clementi, an eighteen-
year-old Rutgers undergraduate who jumped to his death
off the George Washington Bridge after his dorm-mate used
a webcam to observe Clementi's liaison with another young
man. After watching it with a female student in her dorm
room, the roommate reported it on Twitter.

Presumably, the two young spies had no idea that the sen-
sitive Clementi would kill himself, nor apparently any inkling
of how their own devices might be turned against them.
Almost immediately after Clementi's suicide, the story went
viral, with thousands of posted comments on the wicked behavior of the dorm-mates, countered by a host of others de-
crying the stupid overreaction of the outed gay young man.
The same techniques and attitudes that prevented Clementi
from carrying on his love life—and perhaps testing his own
sexual orientation—in peace prevented his betrayers from

paying a penalty appropriate to their youthful trespass. No matter the outcome of the legal charges brought against them, they may never live down what they did. It is a curious paradox of the times we live in, when no commandment is inscribed on tablets of stone but every one of our transgressions lives eternally within some data bank, effectively beyond the pale of forgiveness.

•

America is a pluralistic society in nothing so much as the plurality of ways in which an American's privacy can be breached. By most assessments, the Clementi incident was run-of-the-mill, notable only because of its heartbreaking consequence. Government agencies and private corporations vie with each other to know the most about us—and sometimes join hands out of mutual interest, as Yahoo and Google have done in China. Verizon alone receives 90,000 demands for information from law enforcement agencies every year. Four months after the 2001 passage of the USA Patriot Act—a 340-page document "undermining nearly all of the scant privacy protections adopted by Congress over the last forty years"—4 percent of all U.S. libraries and 11 percent of all libraries in communities of more than 50,000 had been visited by FBI agents requesting information about their patrons' reading habits. The National Security Agency intercepts 1.7 billion e-mails every day.

At the same time, corporations mine our e-mails and Internet searches in the hopes of honing their marketing strategies. No sooner do I press the send button that e-mails a letter of recommendation to a female student or a note of thanks to a female editor and an ad for an online dating service invites me to learn more about a bevy of eligible lovelies "in your area." More than 96 percent of Google's $29 billion in revenue for 2010, a sum exceeding the combined advertising revenues of all newspapers, came from advertisers sold on the search engine's ability to know our individual wants. Unlike Orwell's Big Brother, who merely sought to sniff out dissent, corporate Big Brother wishes to know our every desire, confident that we can be pleasured into submission. And we have hardly seen the worst. Privacy expert Jeffrey Rosen speculates that "it would be a simple enough task for Facebook or Google" to launch an "Open Planet" surveillance system, by "which anyone in the world could log onto the Internet, select a particular street view . . . and zoom in on a particular individual. . . . Most of the architecture for implementing it already exists."

Such a development would be good news not only for the Big Brothers of government and business but also for what Walter Kirn, writing about the Clementi case, calls "Little Brother." He means any nosy individual with an electronic device. With the use of something called a keylogger, for instance, you can keep track of a spouse's computer keystrokes. With the use of Google Images you can change your mind about a blind date. The surveillance state and the surveillance economy are matched by a surveillance culture, each daring the other to go one step further in vandalizing old norms.

The plurality of intrusions on our privacy has the cumulative effect of inducing a sense of helplessness—in much the same way as an exhaustive list of environmental carcinogens can make a person despair of her health. "If one thing doesn't kill you, something else will," says the beleaguered citizen, opening his laptop and unwrapping a hot pastrami sandwich with all the resignation of a condemned man eating his last meal. The most important question raised by the

Tyler Clementi case is not how we can manage to protect our privacy against so many threats, but how we can ever hope to resist our Big Brothers without reliable brothers-in-arms. Solidarity, even more than privacy, is what's at stake. As Tocqueville said, a tyrant does not need his subjects to love him; it is sufficient for his purposes if they hate one another. Perhaps Tocqueville set the bar too high. Mistrust might do the job.

•

I'm pretty sure my friend Ralph did not fully grasp my objections to his sharing my letters without permission. He sounded more perplexed than defensive on the phone. He suggested that perhaps I felt different about the matter than another person would because I am a writer. I balked at this, but not without wondering if he was right.

I'm also pretty sure the two undergraduates who spied on Clementi did not grasp the enormity of what they were doing. Certainly their society did not contribute a great deal to any such understanding. Not long before the young man hooked up his webcam, a school board in Lower Merion, Pennsylvania, was charged with using school-issued laptops to spy on students *in their homes.* As long ago as Watergate, Chairman Mao wondered aloud what Nixon could have done that his people would have found so offensive. "Americans are always playing with tape recorders," he said, and many Americans remain as uncomprehending of "what Nixon did wrong" as Mao was. I can't know this for sure, but it's tempting to believe that the students who spied on Clementi were actually seeking a kind of vindication for their snooping when one of them tweeted what they had done. After all, what Clementi was doing was hidden, whereas they

were "sharing" their deed "out in the open," and isn't openness always good? If they weren't hiding anything, then how
could they be doing anything wrong?

I'm also doubtful if the commentators and court fully
grasped what had happened either. Early in the arraignment
of the accused, a question was raised as to whether Clementi's dorm-mates had witnessed explicit sexual activity or
merely a chaste romantic interlude. One sensed a collective
bated breath as reporters sought to determine just how
steamy the details had been, as if arranging a surreptitious
peek at a young man putting on his deodorant or saying his
prayers or practicing his violin would have been no big deal.
People put that stuff on YouTube all the time.

There was also a prevailing assumption that Clementi had
taken his life because he could not live with the public disclosure of his sexual orientation, a tragedy that might so easily
have been prevented with a vaccination of political correct-
ness. If only he'd realized that *we* didn't have a problem with
his being gay—the more enlightened of us anyway—then *he*
could not possibly have had a problem with our acquiring the
knowledge, *vox populi vox Dei* and all that. In fact, Clementi
had already come out to his family and to a friend. It is far
more plausible to assume that he took his life because he
found the thought of living in a world without privacy un-
bearable. Why else would societies take such pains to punish
theft beyond the requirement of simple restitution if not that
they realize how much their very existence depends on a cov-
enant of trust? Who steals my purse steals trash, but who
steals the confidence with which I take my purse to market
trashes my world.

These basic misconceptions, coupled with personal expe-
riences like the one with Ralph, make me deeply skeptical
of the popular notion that older norms of privacy are being

trampled underfoot by hordes of clueless kids with their diabolical electronic devices. I think those norms have been underfoot for a while. Alan Westin's classic *Privacy and Freedom* was sounding the alarm as far back as 1967. If I didn't know better, I would suppose Facebook had been invented by some boomer layabout with a howdy-there paunch and an unbuttoned Hawaiian shirt, and I will not be surprised if people soon to be in their seventies are still friending each other long after younger folks have put away childish things. When *Harper's Magazine* published the cantankerously pro-privacy essay that led to this book, the ratio of the approving to the disapproving letters I received was about three to one. Interestingly, most of the positives came from young women, and all of the negatives from middle-aged men. I did not find this ironic.

I came of age in the 1960s. Raised by parents who remembered such things as telephone party lines and troop ships, I was taught to value my privacy. The verbal similarity of "minding your business" and "doing your business" (my grandmother's euphemism for going to the toilet) impressed upon me at an early age the connection between privacy and physicality, between private conversations and private parts. Nevertheless, I grew up sensing that privacy was somehow at odds with the times, and that I was too even though I grew my hair long and listened to Dylan like everyone else. Whatever its reputation to the contrary, I remember the sixties as a time of coercive conformity on both sides of the barricades, and it does not surprise me that flower power should have wilted into the decadent stinking blossoms of identity politics and academic dogmatism.

It was the time of *Candid Camera* and the dawn of confessional poetry, a time when people blithely assumed that what the Kinsey Report had revealed about the sexual habits of Americans was surely more comprehensive than the sexual habits of those Americans willing to respond to sex surveys. Weren't they the same thing? It was the time when Andy Warhol assured us of our fifteen minutes of fame, which the Internet would convert to time everlasting. Hippie communes featured such ostentatious details as the centrally placed bathtub of the Aloe Community, and Brotherhood of the Spirit's "toilet city" (several "toilets in a semicircle . . . so everybody got to sit across from each other")—all intended, no doubt, to subvert middle-class hang-ups, though perhaps proving no more than the lengths to which middle-class frivolity can go when permitted to run amok. By the time I'd graduated from college, the Loud family was coming apart on PBS, precursors of reality TV and the ensuing preference for celebrity over citizenship, when voting would come to be associated with voting someone *off*—off the island or the dance floor, out of a job. But this was not new to me either. Sly and the Family Stone said it on "Dance to the Music" before Simon said it on *American Idol,* "All the squares go out."

I wonder how privacy will fare as my contemporaries and I age. Given our zeal for anything we perceive as impacting personal choice, privacy will be high on our list of concerns—or should I say high on our list of pretexts for a grievance. At the same time, with the increasing loneliness of aging and sole survivorship, coupled with my generation's emphasis on "relating," I anticipate a level of intrusiveness and self-exposure that my octogenarian parents would find obscene. I am occasionally taunted by a vision of waiting for my medicine in a nursing home as some fellow inmate shanghais the nurse on duty to hear about his dreams, his lovers, his concerts (the ones he remembers), his experiments in spirituality, and the zodiac signs of all nineteen of his grandchildren—or of trying to navigate my walker down the hall toward a quickly cooling bowl of soup only to be waylaid every ten feet and told I look like I could "use a hug." Physician-assisted suicide may not be a legal option even then, and with global warming well under way, my chances of being adopted by an Arctic Circle tribe and set adrift on an ice floe are depressingly slight.

Sentiments like these seem radically at odds with my political beliefs, which could be described as approximately socialistic, vacillating between social democracy and something in a deeper shade of red. I believe that economies should be planned, that corporations should be worker-owned, and that resources should be managed according to the Marxist principle "from each according to his ability, to each according to his need." At the same time, I admit to feeling visceral revulsion at the mere mention of the word *social*; I cannot hear the word *communal* without thinking of a religious sect reputed to use a common washcloth in place of toilet paper. "You and your closest men friends should form a club," my daughter once said to me when she was still a child. "You'd have only one meeting a year and all of you would refuse to attend it."

I suspect this tension in myself is not unique. I suspect that some version of it exists in the hearts of more than a few Americans. It is certainly at the heart of this book and is one of my main reasons for writing it. For I have come to believe that what feels like a contradiction in my personality need not be a contradiction in political practice. I believe with the writer of one of the Hebrew Psalms that righteousness and peace—that is to say, a society based on economic justice and a peace based on the right to be let alone—can be brought to kiss.

•

As for Ralph and me, we were reconciled easily enough. He had meant me no harm, as I understood from the start, and he eventually came to understand what had so offended me. He asked my pardon. It's possible I will need to ask his pardon after what I've written here; I'm reasonably confident of getting it. We are at the age when one does not take the loss of a friend lightly. As Voltaire said when urged on his deathbed to renounce the devil, "This is no time to be making new enemies."

I will continue to wonder if Ralph was right about our different senses of privacy owing to different occupations—but in his case more than mine. If Ralph is not as inclined as I am to be horrified by breaches of confidence, that may be because his occupation as a medical examiner puts horror on a fairly high threshold. In the penultimate paragraph of last year's Christmas letter he broaches the subject of early retirement by way of telling how profoundly shaken he was by a case involving the seventy-pound body of a fifteen-year-old girl. Cause of death: a combination of starvation and torture at the hands of her parents. The privacy I value so highly, and had accused him of not valuing highly enough, seems not to have done her much good.

3

PENUMBRAS

WHAT IS PRIVACY AND
ARE WE EVEN ABLE TO SAY?

> I love living a private life because I do so by my own choice,
> not because I am unsuited to a public one.
>
> — MONTAIGNE

The first thing we can say by way of defining privacy is that it exists only by choice. In the absence of choice, privacy is merely the privation with which it shares a common linguistic root, just as sex, work, and singing a song become rape, slavery, and humiliation when forced on us against our will. The girl who died a miserable death at the hands of her psychotic parents was not living a private life; she was living in a hell of loneliness. They are not the same thing.

The confusion of privacy and loneliness amounts to the Gordian knot of modern capitalist societies, the big blue bow of alienation on our package of consumer goods. It also bedevils the thinking of capitalism's less imaginative critics, who mistakenly assume that by eliminating everything private they will eliminate loneliness too. I will have more to say about that as we continue. For now, suffice it to say that privacy is either a choice or a lie.

We make a clear choice for privacy whenever we hang the PRIVACY PLEASE sign on the outside of a hotel room door. In some places it reads DO NOT DISTURB, which in essence means the same thing. We hang out the sign because we are not prepared to leave the room, because we are not prepared to have someone else come into the room, and because, at least until checkout time, we feel some claim to call the room our own. Until a less negotiable checkout time, we feel the same claim on our lives.

All of us share that basic understanding. Even the hotel housekeepers, many of them recent immigrants whose languages do not contain a word exactly equivalent to the English word *privacy*—because no language does—can understand the sign. They have been taught to know its meaning in the same way as they have been taught to put their backs to the wall when a paying guest walks by.

Whenever I can afford to stay in a hotel, usually when someone else puts me up in one, I make frequent use of that sign. I enjoy working in hotel rooms, which are like offices with the added amenities of a handy toilet and a phone that never rings. I can work in peace. When any further post-ponement is likely to create anxieties among the staff, I re-verse the sign so that it reads SERVICE REQUESTED. Then I will leave the room. At that point I consider PRIVACY PLEASE addressed to me.

Of course, by leaving the room I put some of my pri-vacy at risk, since there is nothing to prevent the housekeeper from looking through my stuff. But I assume that she has a life and work to do. She is a housekeeper, after all, not a hacker. I also assume that, in this case at least, her need for privacy trumps mine. If I feel it necessary, I can always cover my books and papers, close my laptop, and erase at least a few of the clues as to every single thing I, and my wife if she is with me, have been doing in the room for the past twelve hours. In other words, I can preserve some of our privacy by making the room more publicly presentable to someone else.

This is an aspect of privacy that receives too little atten-tion, I think. Some contend that a concern for privacy be-trays a self-centered value system; I would say that it is our conception of privacy that is self-centered. We speak of it entirely in personal terms, as an act of self-preservation, failing to consider that the protection of one's own privacy is often a gesture of respect to another person's sensibilities.

This is what the English essayist Charles Lamb apparently had in mind when he wrote "A Bachelor's Complaint" against the "pure, unrecompensed, unqualified insult" of married couples' behavior in the company of their single friends. Husbands and wives "perk up" their affections for each other, Lamb writes, "in the faces of us single people so shamelessly." Lamb desires more "ceremony" in order "to take off the uneasy feeling which we derive from knowing ourselves to be less the object of love . . . than some other person is." Inhabitants of a less ceremonious time, we would want to ask old Chuckie what his problem was. We also might find it strange that he is resentful, not of married people's privacy—of their refusal to be obligingly "transparent"—but of their failure to honor their privacy enough, and him into the bargain. In Lamb's view, privacy is a social obligation, owing as much to fellow feeling as to self-respect.

In a different culture but a slightly similar vein, Bedouin women traditionally do not veil their faces when they enter Egyptian cities because they consider Egyptians morally inferior to themselves. One might expect a different response—best use the veil because there's no telling what an Egyptian might get himself up to if he sees a pretty face—but protection is not the point. Bedouin women veil as a gesture of respect to social (usually male) superiors, and Egyptians—like bachelors, in Lamb's view—don't count. Bedouin women do not veil for low-status males either. It goes without saying that if Bedouin women of childbearing age counted for more, the protocols of veiling would be moot (as they are for their female elders).

I imagine that most of the scholars and jurists who have written and ruled on privacy get to spend more time in hotels than I do. At least they get to stay in better hotels. Few of them would make the mistake I made on my first book tour of believing I could save my publisher money by contenting myself with what I took to be the complimentary refreshments provided in the room's minibar. As with the concept of privacy, the basic idea of keeping to a budget was within my grasp, but I had missed some important particulars. This is why we have scholars and jurists.

•

It turns out that not all of them are comfortable about defining privacy, however. "Is privacy a situation, or a value, or a claim of right?" asks legal scholar Kenneth L. Karst. "Is privacy itself the subject of our moral and legal claims, or is it a code word that always stands for some other interest?" According to Tom Gerety, privacy is "like many legal concepts" in that it is "not so much a philosophical conception as a practical one, more readily identified by its messy precedents than by its tidy definition."

Still, one hopes for a working definition, and not necessarily one confined to the outlines of a legal concept. A natural place to look is in the contrast between public and private, though that isn't very tidy either. It is at least readily understandable, in the way that we understand our front yards to be more public and our backyards more private, but a good philosopher or a persistent Jehovah's Witness can easily blur the boundaries. "No human life, not even the life of a hermit," writes Hannah Arendt, "is possible without a world which directly or indirectly testifies to the presence of other human beings." To which we might add that the bustling public world of other human beings stands on the achievements of more than a few hermits.

Public and private are, as one writer calls them, "interdependent chambers of the same heart." The degradation of privacy increasingly bemoaned in the press and in books such as this one can easily be correlated with a degradation of public life, and vice versa. If you were too busy watching *American Idol* to notice when the provisions of the USA Patriot Act were extended, you can expect that quite soon someone may be watching you. But we needn't make the point so grimly. Isn't part of the pleasure of going to a movie, concert, or play the simultaneous awareness of a private experience coupled with a sense of public communion? I suspect that would not have been possible in the Roman Colosseum, even if one had the good fortune of not being included among the entertainments.

Other attempts at definition by way of contrast juxtapose privacy with secrecy, though this approach can also prove dicey. It has been noted that while privacy is a right, secrecy is not; that while privacy lacks any specific content, secrecy is made up of specifics; that whereas privacy has a generally positive connotation, secrecy implies that "other people may have some claim to the hidden information." Sociologists have suggested that while privacy is the prerogative of the powerful, secrecy is the resort of the less powerful, including children, who form the concept of a secret by about the age of four. For most of us, though, the notion of privacy includes the option of keeping secrets, even to the grave.

Some scholars focus on one or another salient aspect of privacy. Given a history that begins with a revolution, and a legal tradition informed by the Bill of Rights, American writers understandably emphasize resistance to governmental intrusion, the sense of a line that authority dare not cross.

Even so entitled an authority as a school principal looking for drugs can be called to account, as in *Safford Unified School District v. Redding* (2009), where the Supreme Court ruled eight to one against the strip search of a wrongfully accused high school student. At the same time, Julie Inness's seminal book on privacy (*Privacy, Intimacy, and Isolation,* 1992) emphasizes intimacy as "the common denominator that internally organizes and externally links tort and constitutional privacy law." In short: "Privacy protects love, care, and liking." It's worth a reflective pause to marvel at a value associated with such seemingly disparate elements as intimacy and resistance, though this is perhaps no surprise to anyone who has fought hard and loved well.

Privacy is complex enough to have inspired several cluster definitions. Alan Westin identifies four constituent elements: solitude, intimacy, anonymity, and reserve. Anita Allen speaks of three basic forms: accessibility, seclusion, and anonymity; Judith DeCew, of three basic areas that privacy protects: information, bodily integrity, and expression. In *Whalen v. Roe* (1977), the Supreme Court identified two kinds of interests in privacy cases: "One is the individual interest in avoiding disclosure of personal matters and another is the interest in independence in making certain kinds of important decisions." These interests correspond to the *informational privacy* and *decisional privacy* sometimes found in discussions of the concept.

Almost two decades before *Whalen,* in 1960, jurist William L. Prosser attempted to summarize the various privacy cases that had come before U.S. courts up until that time. He identified four types of privacy invasion: "intrusion upon the plaintiff's seclusion or solitude, or into his private affairs; public disclosure of embarrassing facts about the plaintiff; publicity which places the plaintiff in a false light in the public eye; and appropriation, for the defendant's advantage, of the plaintiff's name or likeness." Prosser's list is worth memorizing; beyond its potential to impress a game show host or a date with a law degree, it can serve as a mental checklist, a kind of "Miranda rights" to be recited whenever we suspect our privacy has been illegally arrested.

Not everyone who addresses privacy is inclined to define it in the abstract. Taking his cue from Prosser and from Ludwig Wittgenstein's idea of family resemblances, according to which "certain concepts might not have a single common characteristic" but rather "draw from a common pool of similar elements," legal scholar Daniel Solove suggests that instead of "attempting to locate the common denominator" of those activities threatened by the loss of privacy, "we should conceptualize privacy by focusing on the specific types of disruption." These types include technological disruptions that did not exist when Prosser formulated his list.

Though Solove's approach strikes me as sound, not least of all because it recapitulates the inductive process by which the right of privacy was historically derived, I can't resist taking a stab at the kind of core definition that Solove warns us—wisely, I think—is doomed to fail.

I would ground privacy in a creaturely resistance to being used against one's will. You can change *used* to *exploited* if you like, but I prefer *used* and add the following qualifications. First, it does not matter how one is used—and in fact, the more intangible the use (as an entertainment for the curious, as a taste of revenge for the envious, as a shortcut in examination protocols for the busily overbooked doctor or nurse), the more likely one is to regard it as a breach of privacy, as opposed to the rougher uses of theft and assault. Second, it does not matter if the exploited person is aware of being used, though it certainly hurts more if she is.

I like my definition for three reasons, and I dislike it for two. I like it, first of all, because its legal relevance is on a par with my legal expertise—nil in both cases. I also like it because it counters the notion that privacy is somehow anti-social. To be used is to be cheated out of one's ability to serve, as slaves are cheated out of it, along with all but a few shreds of their privacy. For example, I cannot serve you with a compliment if you've already spied it in my diary. To be free is not simply to do whatever you want, but also to be able to do some things you might *not* want, but which love, loyalty, or principle inspire you to do. In short, to be free from use is to be free to serve.

Finally, I like my definition because it takes a poke at the flabby morality of insisting that "anything you do is okay so long as it doesn't hurt somebody else" (with the hurt almost never defined by the somebody else). According to that morality, I am doing nothing wrong if I make a clandestine movie of my neighbors having sex, so long as they never find out about it and so long as I reserve the film exclusively for my own enjoyment. According to my definition, I have indeed done something wrong: I have violated my neighbors' privacy. I have used them.

What I dislike about my definition is that it is insufficiently materialistic. I agree with Iris Marion Young, who observes that "much theoretical discussion of privacy seems rather 'virtual,'" giving the impression that "privacy is largely cognitive or mental." She prefers to focus on "the *material bases* of privacy," on the fact that "even my thoughts are fleeting unless I give them some sort of expressive embodiment—a card, a diagram, a photograph." I hope to give more emphasis to embodiment later on.

What troubles me even more about the definition is that it compels me to ask self-incriminating questions about the work I do as a writer, in which the need for material often involves the freewheeling use of real persons as subjects. I'm sure my definition has other, more substantive flaws. I certainly hope so, and for reasons that go well beyond the challenge to my conscience.

•

The difficulties in defining privacy ought rather to encourage than depress us. If privacy has to do with our essential humanity—if it is "an individual's moral title to his existence," as Jeffrey Reiman calls it, if it allows us to maintain "our very integrity as persons," as Charles Fried argues— then should we be dismayed if its meaning proves to be as resistant to oversimplification as that of the person sleeping beside us? What preserves mystery might also be mysterious.

As if in rebuttal to that thought, I have just noticed on the jacket of one of the books I've quoted an endorsement written by a legal scholar, claiming that the author, also a legal scholar, is "committed to demystifying 'the right to privacy.'" But this means no more than that the author and his endorser are committed to doing their jobs. I don't tell lawyer jokes, and if I ever go to court to defend my right to privacy, I hope to have counsel more like Clarence Darrow than Saint John of the Cross. I don't want a mystical decision, I want a favorable one.

Outside of court, however, I appreciate mystery; in fact, it is a key ingredient in my private life, in my intimate associations, and in just about everything I would call beautiful—a category that includes Supreme Court Justice William O. Douglas's words in *Griswold v. Connecticut* (1965), a landmark decision for privacy rights and reproductive freedom. Writing for the majority, which ruled that a government ban on the sale of contraceptives was unconstitutional, Douglas said "specific guarantees in the Bill of Rights have penumbras, formed by emanations from those guarantees that help give them life and substance."

This turns out to be perfectly acceptable legal language, but the last time I read anything quite like it was in the mystical writings of Plotinus. Not every legal scholar has found Douglas's approach as edifying as I do, and even I have a slight caveat. With all due respect to the Justice, I would suggest that the Bill of Rights derives from the "penumbras," rather than the other way around. By that I mean that the penumbras are most properly located around you and me. They were certainly located around William O. Douglas. If you look closely, you might even glimpse a few emanating from the Somali housekeeper who cleans your hotel toilet for slave wages, though on that score even the most libertarian Westerner generally prefers to have his women veiled.

4

GETTING YOUR DEGREE
THE PURITY CODE OF THE
AMERICAN PUBLIC SQUARE

What a heavy burden is a name that has become too
famous.   —VOLTAIRE

In 1975 one of those heroic bystanders we all hope we will
either be in a crisis or have standing next to us in a crisis
stepped decisively forward and knocked an assassin's gun
off its mark. The target was Gerald Ford, then president of
the United States. His savior was Oliver Sipple, an out gay
man. But not so out as he was soon going to be.

Neither Sipple's parents nor his siblings knew that he was
gay, and he had not wanted them to know. They found out
when the *San Francisco Chronicle* made his sexual orientation public and other national papers quickly followed up
on the story. Of course, *quickly* needs to be taken relative to
the media capabilities of 1975. Today the revelation would be
as instantaneous as the gunshot that almost killed Ford.

Sipple sued for invasion of privacy and lost. The court explained its verdict by noting that Sipple was already prominent in the gay community and a frequent patron in gay bars.
His face and name had also appeared in more than one publication with a gay readership. Therefore, the court concluded,
the facts of his sexuality could not be construed as private.
The decision was in marked contrast to a 1985 French case in
which a man who had marched in a Paris gay pride parade
(reportedly dressed in a conspicuously proud manner) was
legally able to oppose publication of his photograph. As law

professor James Q. Whitman explains, "to the French way of thinking, the fact that one has revealed oneself to a restricted public—say, the gay community of Paris—does not imply that one has lost all protections before the larger public."

Clearly that is not the American way of thinking; at least it wasn't in the case of Sipple, even though he had not been proclaiming his sexual orientation when he'd acted on behalf of President Ford, whom he seems to have regarded as mortally endangered rather than irresistibly cute. Like other cases it resembles, the Sipple decision puts additional nuances on the definitions advanced in the previous chapter, especially in regard to the complex relationship between public and private, and especially in their American context.

The court that ruled against Sipple apparently did not feel that his right to privacy included "the control of one's public image," an idea that "has long appealed to the most philosophically sophisticated American commentators," according to Whitman, but not always to the nation's highest courts. Jeffrey Rosen notes that the Supreme Court "has come close to saying we have no legitimate expectations of privacy in public places"—unless, as Justice Harlan wrote in *Katz v. United States* (1967), a person exhibits "an actual subjective expectation of privacy" which is "one that society is prepared to recognize as 'reasonable.'" (In the case of *Katz*, the "reasonable" expectation was that the FBI would not have planted a recording device on the outside of a telephone booth.)

Harlan's qualification fails to take into account two significant factors, or so it seems to me. The first is the number of people whose very act of stepping out the front door represents a "subjective expectation of privacy"—because the public sphere is the only place where they can have a reasonable hope of finding it. As the nineteenth-century feminist Charlotte Gilman Perkins testily observed, "The home is the one place on earth where no one of the component individuals can have any privacy."

The second factor is the ease with which the "subjective expectation of privacy" is allowed to be trumped by an objective but entirely unforeseen calamity. In other words, it is almost as if Mr. Sipple "got what he deserved" by acting decisively in a crisis. A 1929 court said as much when a woman named Lillian Jones "heroically attacked" two men who stabbed her husband to death as the couple was strolling through Louisville, Kentucky, and then sued for invasion of privacy when a newspaper printed her and her husband's pictures. (Mr. Jones was lucky in his marriage if in nothing else.) A person forfeits "the right to live one's life in seclusion," the court ruled, when he or she "willingly or not, becomes an actor in an occurrence of public or general interest."

It's a toss-up which phrase is the more chilling, "willingly or not" or "general interest." In 1982 a woman was abducted, stripped naked, and terrorized in an apartment. Police managed to free her from her kidnapper and hurried her to safety as she clutched a hastily grabbed dish towel to her exposed body. A newspaper published a photograph of her escape the next day. A sympathetic jury awarded her a total of $10,000 in damages when she sued for invasion of privacy, but a Florida court overturned the decision on appeal. The court deemed the photograph a "newsworthy" and apparently indispensable ingredient in what it called "a typical exciting emotion-packed drama to which newspeople, and others, are attracted." Presumably "others" includes individuals who lack only the guts to abduct and terrorize women on their own initiative.

Court decisions like these suggest that the right of privacy *in public,* like a life insurance policy, can be granted only to people who meet certain norms. The safe, the solvent, and the healthy—in short, the "lucky"—fall within the charmed circle of those protected. Get yourself raped, blown up, or diagnosed with AIDS or cancer and the deal is off. The wounded African American soldier carried out of a bombed Beirut compound with his buttocks exposed, the Russian hostage gassed in a rescue mission against Chechen separatists, caught by photographer Justin Sutcliffe propped against a bus window with her face contorted in an ecstasy of delirium and one of her breasts fully bared, are not lucky—and in some deeply disturbing way, "not us." Their misfortunes have sullied them somehow, turned them into exhibitions. They have joined the ranks of the Hottentot Venus, an African slave named Saartjie Baartman who was forced to display her voluptuous buttocks as a curiosity throughout Europe. If they didn't want people looking at their tits and asses, they ought to have kept themselves out of danger.

The rationale amounts to a de facto purity code—not unlike the one that justifies tearing the clothes off a woman journalist because if she has shown her face so brazenly on the streets of Cairo she can hardly have an objection to showing everything else—and it manifests in strange ways. Consider *Veronia School District 47J v. Acton* (1995), in which the Supreme Court ruled that high school athletes could not object to mandatory drug testing on the grounds that they had voluntarily subjected themselves to "communal undress" when they took showers. In short, their privacy was less than virginal. It was no longer pure.

Or consider the no less bizarre 1986 Louisiana court case that reduced the damages awarded by a lower court to women who'd had their breasts, rectums, and vaginas examined by an unauthorized National Guard recruiter who took it upon himself to administer the bogus "physicals." The $8,500 per plaintiff was "clearly" excessive, the court ruled, reducing the amount by more than half. After all, the women "were adults, one was married, and two of the four had children." To distinguish the logic of the court's ruling from the logic that once disqualified "promiscuous" or "alluringly" dressed women from bringing charges for rape requires keener powers of analysis than I possess.

•

Fortunately, a few observations lie within easier reach. Since most of them will figure in subsequent chapters, it is probably a good idea to lay them out now.

The first and probably the most obvious is the way in which some of the rulings cited above represent a restriction of freedom—the freedom, for example, to rescue a president, take a call from your proud and blissfully ignorant mother (*I bet there's a nice girl out there who'd be thrilled to date a real hero*), beat a couple of ridiculously ignorant homophobes in a few games of handball, and then meet your lover for a night of barhopping and ironical congratulations in the underground scene of your choice. It has been posited that American privacy is a liberty-based concept, as opposed to the dignity-based version favored by the French and most Europeans. Here in the Land of the Free, we like to think of our privacy in "decisional" terms, and we suspect it whenever it seems in danger of impinging on other cherished freedoms, such as the First Amendment freedom of the press (and the press photographer). *Freedom*—that's the word.

But what is freedom for most of us if not determining the *relative degree* of otherwise fairly generic decisions? Many of our choices are not so much matters of *what* as of *how*, not whether to have lunch but where and when. They are not nouns so much as adverbs. That would seem to be the insight of those pivotal privacy cases having to do with reproductive rights—*Griswold v. Connecticut* (1965) and *Roe v. Wade* (1973)—that although many women are capable and even desirous of bearing children, this does not mean that a woman's only options are entering a convent or becoming the Old Woman in the Shoe. By extension, there ought to be degrees of privacy between complete anonymity and total exposure. And there are—for some of us.

Another notable feature of the precariousness of privacy in public is the economic subtext. More often than not, *newsworthy* means capable of being sold as news. The hallowed right to know sugars off as somebody else's right to make a buck. My neighbor Robert Gensberg, an attorney who represents a man imprisoned at Guantánamo Bay since 2002, still cannot get a straight answer as to whether his phone was tapped, but he does have a right to know the name of the guy Jennifer Lopez took along on her last romantic getaway. By law I am not permitted to know which of the foods at the supermarket have been genetically engineered, and hence am not able to exercise the "consumer choice" that we are repeatedly reminded is all that separates us from the lower mammals and the North Koreans, but the knowledge of other, more "newsworthy" matters, such as the color of the panties an office worker might be wearing under her dress should she ever have to jump from a burning building, is the inalienable right of a free and sovereign people.

Not surprisingly, one's chances of success in a breach of privacy suit are increased if one can claim a monetary loss. In *Zacchini v. Scripps-Howard Broadcasting Co.* (1977), a "human cannonball" prevailed against the First Amendment defense of a television network that had filmed and broadcast his act without payment. The Supreme Court ruled that the broadcast was "the appropriation of the very activity by which the entertainer acquired his reputation." One wonders if the woman hostage in the 1982 suit against the newspaper might have prevailed in court had she been a professional stripper and thus able to claim that her commoditized nudity had been "appropriated." Along the same lines, consider *Lewis v. Dayton* (1983), in which a Michigan court ruled that a retailer had avoided violating its customers' privacy by posting signs to warn the wary and the literate that the fitting rooms were under surveillance. While the store ran the risk of losing innumerable pairs of pants worth, say, seventy-five dollars apiece (slightly less where I buy mine), all the customer had to lose was his dignity, which, whatever certain credit card advertisements might have to say about sentimental attachments, is not "priceless." If it can't be priced, it's worthless.

No less significant in this "purity code" is the implication that life in public is inherently sullied. The statement may seem counterintuitive: Don't we keep our dirty laundry private and hang the clean articles out in the sun? While this is certainly true of socks and secrets, it is not necessarily true of privacy. Like the ideal femininity with which it has historically been associated, privacy is "pure"; life in public—like politics, money, and sex—is a filthy thing. Of course on some level that suits us. It certainly suits the imperatives of the market. If lucre is filthy, then we're free to do every filthy thing imaginable with it. Pigs in shit needn't bother to be too fastidious, which is why we say they're as happy as pigs in shit.

The filth is more likely to rub off on those with less opportunity to get out of the sty. Social class is defined in large part by the degree of freedom one has to move between private space and public space, and by the amount of time one spends in relative privacy. Do you drive to work or do you take the subway? Do you work mostly with colleagues and clients or with customers and taxpayers? How often do you feel your body jostled in the course of a day? Is your workspace known as the inner sanctum, or the fishbowl? The degree to which a person is free to control his or her public exposure corresponds to that person's degree in the ancient sense of "place in society," as when Macbeth tells his dinner guests, "You know your own degrees"—that is, you know how close to me you're entitled to sit. If Jeffrey Rosen is correct in saying that the Supreme Court has come close to declaring that we have no legitimate expectation of privacy in public places, then he is talking more about the daily experience of the woman who works at the minimart where I get my gas than he is about her favorite customer.

It goes without saying that cyberspace has become another "filthy" dimension of public space, although, as the dates of some of the legal cases cited here indicate, the issue of degree is older than the Internet. Still, the Internet has done much to narrow the spectrum between utterly unknown and totally out there. The idea of taking your songs to a small coffeehouse and trying them out on a few sympathetic listeners before setting your sights on the Newport Folk Festival has gone the way of the Kingston Trio. Newport draws a few thousand at best, while YouTube gets over a billion visitors a day, and anyone sitting in the coffeehouse with an iPhone in her hemp tote bag can put you on YouTube. "I won't be happy till I'm as famous as God," Madonna said, but you don't have to be God or even Madonna to achieve a global presence not only beyond your wildest dreams but quite possibly beyond your control.

This occurs not only in space but in time—one is tempted to say in eternity. The Library of Congress is preserving Tweets. One wonders how long it will be before there are national repositories for faux pas, belches, farts—unzipped flies preserved as if in amber for aeons. Supposedly ours is an age of mind-numbing change, perpetual self-invention, everything morphing nanosecond by nanosecond, yet we have come to be as frozen in our moments as a mastodon in ice. In 1964 a woman in Alabama successfully sued a newspaper for printing a photograph of her skirts being lifted by air jets outside a carnival funhouse. The camera had turned what would otherwise have been a fleeting moment of embarrassment—or perhaps a delicious moment of scandal, the forty-four-year-old wife of a chicken farmer transported to the Moulin Rouge, for just a few heartbeats and a handful of admiring fans—into a stuffed and mounted conversation piece for thousands of dinner tables. What so horrified the woman—she was reportedly given to crying jags after the photo appeared—would strike many as a relic from gentler times. On the Internet, which features special sites for voyeuristic "upskirt" photo shots, Flora Bell Graham's exposure outside an Alabama funhouse would be as everlastingly preserved as Stonehenge or Monica Lewinsky's semen-stained dress. The fairy-tale scenario in which spellbound humans are locked in the poses of their last carefree moment is coming true.

·

If any of the foregoing observations have produced an uneasy sense of what is best left unsaid, a disquiet that people in more reverent ages would have felt in the presence of a perceived blasphemy, then the reader has intuited a final relevant factor to this discussion. I refer to the ubiquitous prissy rectitude that attaches to any topic sanctified by the labels of information, openness, or transparency. Privacy, some would like to claim, is a retrograde Victorian value, but the Victorianism of our times is anything but private. We should take a look at that too.

5

PRUDERY 2.0

From the place where we are right
flowers will never grow.

—YEHUDA AMICHAI

In 1998 a scandal involving then president of the United
States Bill Clinton and White House aide Monica Lewinsky
unleashed what American novelist Philip Roth memorably
called "America's oldest communal passion, historically perhaps its most treacherous and subversive pleasure: the ecstasy
of sanctimony."

Ecstasy there was, and sanctimony in abundance, though
I am not sure that Roth saw the sanctimony for what it was.
I do not believe, as he seemed to, that it boiled down to a
puritanical distaste for the president's sexual transgressions, though certainly that played a part. I think the sanctimony had to do instead with a disavowal of prudery so
extreme as to become a reverse form of the same: an unre-
flectively pious regard for the virtues of openness and the
public's "right to know" anything and everything except
what it needs to know in order to fulfill its role as a democratic electorate.

To put the matter another way, the sanctimony had to do
with the world's most powerful man, and a Rhodes scholar
to boot, apparently feeling that he had no viable options for
answering impertinent questions about his sex life other
than to lie about it or reveal it, except perhaps the option of
doing both, which is the one he chose. Given the nature of

the particular sanctimony he was up against, he may have chosen prudently.

At least at the end he was sincere, you see, and sincerity counted for more than any sexual shenanigans. It even counted for more—and this was the part I never figured out, the part where Roth may have been closer to the mark—than the allegation that as governor of Arkansas Clinton had ordered a woman brought to him *in a police car.* But that bit was too close to a legitimate public interest in political power and its abuses, the dirty stuff that prudery, be it antique or modern, holds itself aloof from. Better to concentrate on the authenticity of the president's heart, and on whatever undisclosed detail made his penis look so "unusual."

One can argue, and I do, that we have become as sanctimonious in our zeal to expose and reveal as any "repressed" Victorian was to conceal and deny. We are no less self-righteous, conformist, and cruel. We maintain that we are merely being democratic, that a free and open society demands that we be free with one another's privacy and open to one another's gaze. In his twentieth-century adaptation of Euripides' *Medea*, Robinson Jeffers has his heroine suggest as much: "I understand well enough / That nothing is ever private in a Greek city; whoever withholds anything / Is thought sullen or proud . . . undemocratic / I think you call it."

The political theorist Judith Shklar would call it something else. She writes that "the democracy of everyday life . . . does not arise from sincerity," but rather from citizens' hiding enough of themselves to make social intercourse tenable. She points to a figure such as Benjamin Franklin, who saw nothing amiss in trying to "make himself acceptable to his fellow citizens" by hiding "much of his native character." She warns against "the unending game of mutual unmasking," which has the ironic effect of raising "the general level of sham." In such a game, "any attempt to hide one's feelings, every social formality, role, or ritual, even failures to recognize one's character and possibilities are called acts of hypocrisy or self-betrayal." Rather shockingly, Shklar concludes that "we ought to give up not only our obsession with openness, but indeed go beyond the traditional horror of the hypocrite. . . . Hypocrisy is one of the few vices that bolsters liberal democracy."

If this does indeed shock us, that may be because we have perverted what Elaine Scarry describes as "the Constitutional requirement that people's lives be private and the work of government officials be public." In Scarry's view that requirement was "turned upside down" by the 2001 passage of the USA Patriot Act, which makes "the population *visible* and the Justice Department *invisible*" and "crafts a set of conditions in which our inner lives become transparent, and the workings of the government become opaque."

The question remains as to whether the Patriot Act represented a constitutional innovation so much as a codification of cultural norms already in place. Principal deputy director of national intelligence Donald Kerr argued for the latter when he said that Americans needed to "redefine" their privacy and cited MySpace and Facebook as examples that they had already done so. A good Republican, he apparently did not feel comfortable invoking the prior compliance of President Clinton.

•

No doubt our prudery is based in part on the therapeutic trope of the healing power of self-disclosure. In that case, it is also based on a misunderstanding. Despite Freud's emphasis on openness, some evidence suggests that patients who self-censor their revelations have a better success rate in therapy than those who compulsively tell all. Possibly this is because they develop better relationships with their therapists. They feel they are seen in a better light and are thus more comfortable disclosing information essential to their treatment. Psychologist Anita Kelly urges patients to "focus on themes as opposed to details," thus disqualifying herself for hosting television talk shows or consulting on any film depicting a session of psychotherapy.

It may be, too, that some of the new prudery derives from the coming-out phase of gay liberation and its partial dislodgment of one of the old prudery's cornerstones. By outing themselves, and in some cases one another, gay and lesbian rebels moved themselves and their society forward—so goes the received narrative, and who would deny the core truth of it? Those of us who are straight, however, and who appropriate the phrase *coming out* (as in the more cultic expressions of "breast cancer survivorship") as glibly as some whites claim to have been treated like "niggers," probably cannot fathom how complicated coming out could be. Even so bold and notorious a figure as the philosopher Michel Foucault was reportedly ambivalent about making his homosexuality public. As noted by Eve Kosofsky Sedgwick, gay and lesbian persons were often caught in "an excruciating system of double binds" in which disclosure was "at once compulsory and forbidden." She cites the 1973 case of an eighth-grade teacher who was removed from his classroom when it became known he was gay, and then was fired when he spoke to the media about his plight. In the several court rulings and appeals that followed his bringing suit against the school district, he was faulted by one court for bringing too much attention to his sexuality and by another for failing to disclose his membership in a college gay society on his job application—even though the school district admitted that had he done so, he would never have been hired.

The teacher's predicament underscores how hard it can be to negotiate your right to privacy when other rights are denied. It also underscores the inadequacy of any sanctimonious notions of "openness" in the absence of equality. In an essay on practical jokes, the poet W. H. Auden speaks of the human "capacity for self-disclosure" that "implies an equal capacity for self-concealment." "Of an animal," he writes by way of contrast, "it is equally true to say that it is incapable of telling us what it really feels, and that it is incapable of hiding its feelings." Oppression attempts to reduce human capabilities to those of an animal—or lower still, to the level where a human being lacks an animal's ability to even know what he feels. How does the French Muslim woman commanded by her religion to wear a head scarf and prohibited by the laws of her adoptive country from wearing a head scarf even know for sure what *she* wants to wear on her head? Shall I be a heretic today or a collaborator?

The insistence on veiling seems oppressive to Westerners, and to me, though I wonder how much our censure of it has to do with concern for the rights of women and how much has to do with no less prudish and patriarchal mores regarding a woman's *obligation* to expose her body for public appraisal: her legs (they better be shaved), her hair (it better be styled), her cleavage (there better be no babies attached lower down). Cultures oblige women to be modest, condemning them for what they let show, or attractive, judging them on the quality of what they are compelled to show. Or on the inferred quality of what they are presumably too ashamed to show. The hackneyed argument of surveillance states is always that "those with nothing to hide have nothing to fear." Patriarchal societies ensure that women always have something of both.

•

Even more than *openness,* the byword of the new prudery is *information*; its favorite motto, "Knowledge is power." You know you are in the presence of a confirmed knowledge-is-power type when your concerns about technologically enhanced surveillance are countered by the assertion that the same technologies are allowing citizens to watch the watchers. "Just the other day," you will be told, "some kid with a smartphone got pictures of these cops beating the crap out of a guy, and now they're all over the Internet!" I've gotten into the habit of remaining silent long enough for the speaker to grasp the implications of what he's just said, but that can leave you speechless for the better part of a week. So what you're telling me, I want to say, is that after more than two hundred years of constitutional government, police are still beating the crap out of citizens, but you feel empowered because somebody took a picture of it?

I don't dispute that knowledge can lead to power or that access to information is essential to self-government, but I fear we have been bamboozled into believing that knowledge is *itself* power, that sitting in a coffee shop racking up "badges" for your visits to muckraking websites makes you a revolutionary. For almost a decade now we have had the *knowledge* that there were never any weapons of mass destruction in Iraq, and I challenge anyone to stand with me next to the bed of a legless twenty-five-year-old Iraq War veteran and tell me that the knowledge was power. Power for whom?

In fact, the only sphere in which the mere possession of knowledge amounts to power is the sphere of individual privacy. If I know that my government has engaged in illegal wiretaps, that knowledge by itself is nothing but an illusion of power—and an illusion that the powerful may be quite happy for me to have. But if I know my neighbor is cheating on his wife, and he knows that I know, *that* is power, however pathetic and humiliating. Perhaps that is one reason for the voyeuristic streak in our culture: a bid for some kind of power on the part of otherwise impotent Peeping Toms. A sense of powerlessness might also explain the bravado with which some people accept that privacy is dead. You hear the same bravado in regard to dire predictions about the environment. *Global warming? Doesn't bother me—I like the heat. Privacy breaches? Let 'em look. I've got nothing to be ashamed of.* Our most abject surrenders occur behind a pretense of indifference.

•

I chose the epigraph for this chapter intending to suggest the moral sterility of that hard, unyielding ground where exposure is always thought to be virtuous and privacy always implies having something nasty to hide. Increasingly in our culture that is "the place where we are right," the place where sanctimony insists on revelation. It is also the place where "flowers will never grow"—including the flowers of self-disclosure, which can flourish only in the absence of coercion and in an atmosphere of trust. What can make a person feel more friendless than being goaded to confession with the words "We're all friends here"?

But it is in the nature of prudery to have things all one way or the other, and so a prudish reading of Amichai's lines will take them to an extreme. It will take them as meaning there is really *no such thing* as a place where we are right. I disagree. There is indeed such a place, small but incontrovertible, and its name is privacy. In the midst of what my friends and associates have a right to expect of me, and the proper claims my nation and my neighbors might lay upon me, is a sphere I have no obligation to reveal for anyone's use. Not even to the Congress of the United States and not even if I am the president of the United States. In the place where I am right, nobody has any business looking for flowers.

6

STANDING UP FOR PRIVACY
A CONTRARIAN ARGUMENT

> To realize the relative validity of one's convictions and yet
> stand for them unflinchingly is what distinguishes a civi-
> lized man from a barbarian.
>
> —JOSEPH SCHUMPETER,
> *CAPITALISM, SOCIALISM AND DEMOCRACY*

Perhaps the single best way to defend privacy against its neo-
prudish critics is to list every value they cherish and to defend those values instead. Transparency, openness, access to
information, community, uninhibited exuberance—none of
them exist to any meaningful degree without privacy as a
precondition. They are either born in the creative incubation
of privacy or depend on a contrast with privacy for their fullest effect. Conspire to remove privacy altogether from the
world, and you will still need enough privacy in which to
hatch your plot.

I am perhaps most aware of privacy in those places where
the Supreme Court has said I have the least right to expect it.
The thrill of visiting New York, which would exist for me
even if no one was waiting there to pay for my lunch, is
largely the frisson of so many privacies jostling together in a
public place. "There are eight million stories in the naked
city," went the closing line of a television series in my childhood. "This has been one of them." But what of the other
seven million, nine hundred and ninety-nine thousand,
nine hundred and ninety-nine? That was what made the line
so powerful, what makes the naked city so wonderful: It isn't

naked at all. Behind millions of inscrutable windows, behind the sunglasses of millions of pedestrians on the move,
are stories I will never hear.

It makes perfect sense to me that apocalypse be imagined
as a time "when every secret is revealed" and every sinner
stands naked, or as a cinematic nightmare in which an im-
posingly public monster attacks New York, shaking people
out of their taxicabs and private thoughts. It is the same outcome either way, nothing less than the end of the world.

There are many reasons to stand up for privacy, some
having to do with building a good society, others having to
do with living a tolerable life. Given the larger concerns
of this book, I will concentrate on the former. But first I want
to acknowledge the mere pleasure of privacy, of being able to
reveal myself or have someone reveal herself to me utterly
without compulsion. Of walking through Times Square deli-
ciously high on the knowledge that there are millions of stories I will never know and, even if I were granted the power to
know them, would refuse to know as a matter of principle.

•

A second way to defend privacy, especially as a political value,
is to grant the truth of the worst that can be said about it:
that it is selfish. *Si*, the Chinese word that may come closest
to the English word *privacy*, means approximately that. Chinese is wise on that score. The right of privacy implies that
an individual human being is so important that he or she is
entitled to an inviolable sphere of self-interest. Without that
recognition, democracy is merely rule by a multitude of petty
tyrants, and altruism little more than a benign form of
harassment.

But if one accepts a right to be selfish, it follows that others have that same right; otherwise it is not a *right* at all, but

merely a whim. The beauty of privacy, when it is beautiful, is that the most radical acceptance of our own prerogatives leads us to an empathetic sense of "the others." No less than ourselves, they are entitled to be let alone. The sage goes into the mountains, turning his back on society and all of its obligations, only to return and proclaim the Golden Rule.

We might go so far as to say that there is a "vaccination effect" to privacy: it provides some immunity even to those members of the population who refuse the vaccine. In an extreme example of that refusal, Berliner Christian Heller has undertaken to live what he calls "a post-privacy life" by maintaining a live wiki in which he exposes every detail of his daily existence on the Internet. He has posted a link to his bank account; you can read the details of his morning toilette. "This transparency that we live in—more and more we can't avoid that," he says, so we have to confront the loss of our privacy "head-on." Presumably Mr. Heller wishes to prove that this is possible, though all he may have proven in the end is that even a stunt like his is bearable thanks to people so invested in their own privacy, and so respectful of his, that they have no interest in gawking at his life or taking full advantage of its obsessive revelations.

For most of us privacy provides a refuge from the world. Christopher Lasch speaks of domestic life as "a private retreat from a public world increasingly dominated by the impersonal mechanisms of the market." Others might see it as a retreat from a world increasingly dominated by the likes of Christian Heller. T. S. Eliot said that "human kind / Cannot bear very much reality"; often the reality we cannot bear very much of is humankind. Sartre put it tersely: "Hell is other people."

Here, too, the self-regard of privacy can pay social dividends. Judith Shklar speaks of the danger to liberal societies posed by misanthropy, which can overtake us "if we contemplate dishonesty, infidelity, and cruelty, especially, for too long a time." Seen in that light, privacy can be regarded as a break in the contemplation. Granted, the media's invasion of our private lives has done as much to make us misanthropic as anything we're likely to observe in the public square, though I would question whether a person glued to her television screen provides the best example of privacy in action. The word applies only if she feels at liberty to turn the TV off. And perhaps to invite a neighbor over for tea. Heaven also is other people.

We have a tendency to think of privacy too much in terms of solitude, although solitude is a part of it. In the darkness of solitude the seeds of genius are able to germinate; we need only think of the number of religious and political movements that began with their founders in retreat, in the wilderness, in exile, in jail. But as much as privacy is about freedom from interference, it is also about what legal scholar Kenneth Karst calls "the freedom of intimate association," the freedom to form "a collective individuality with a life of its own." Without that freedom, a founder founds nothing. Political bodies begin with embryos just as physical bodies do.

Small social units and solitude continue to be important even when a body politic is fully formed, especially if its body type is democratic. Privacy provides a zone of reflection and discussion in which gentler, less forward personalities can have some hope of making a contribution. It gives temporary asylum to those who know themselves to be impressionable, a space to regroup and get their bearings. Writing on privacy and pedagogy, Max van Manen and Bas Levering point out that students will periodically exhibit a need to withdraw from their teachers' attention, influence, and interpretations. The wider applications of that need are obvious; the democratic implications, no less so. This is where those who speak of the elitism of privacy are either dim-witted or disingenuous. Like their close cousins, those who would "subvert hierarchies," they seem motivated by the confidence that with fewer restrictions on their own powers they will find it easier to take charge. It isn't hierarchy they oppose so much as any hierarchy in which they're not the top dogs. Their pretense of egalitarianism is in fact social Darwinism. Privacy amounts to the breather they don't want others to have, the opportunity to detach oneself from the pack and from the demagogue who leads it.

On that score, we might credit privacy not only with enabling us to escape the demagogue but also with helping us to discern him. Often he is someone who seems to *require* publicity and public reassurance, exemplifying Dietrich Bonhoeffer's pointed warning: "Let him who cannot be alone beware of community." We are better led by someone who fears being overwhelmed by community. "The longer I live and the more I see of public men," John Adams wrote to a friend, "the more I wish to be a private one." That went double for his retiring colleague Thomas Jefferson. When we look at political figures like Adams and Jefferson, as well as Montaigne, Dag Hammarskjöld, Elizabeth Cady Stanton, Nelson Mandela, and Václav Havel, what we find is an appreciation of private life that nurtures rather than undercuts their ability to serve publicly. Writing of Havel and his circle, his biographer Eda Kriseová says, "they did not want to be politicians"—perhaps the best qualification a man or woman can have to be one.

A leader disposed toward privacy may be more inclined to resist absolute power if only because privacy does the same. Americans speak of their system of government as one of checks and balances, but the ultimate check on government as a whole is its inability to know everything about those it governs. Agnosticism about the people, as much as faith in them, upholds a democracy.

Some have suggested we'd be better off with neither the agnosticism nor the faith. The utilitarian philosopher Jeremy Bentham wrote in his 1791 book *Panopticon* (the name of his design for a prison in which inmates are kept under perpetual surveillance): "To be incessantly under the eyes of the inspector is to lose in effect the power to do evil and almost the thought of wanting to do it." From the perspective of the twenty-first-century surveillance state, Bentham was ahead of his time. Recently Peter Singer published an essay on "ethics in a world without secrets," in which he defends Bentham by citing a recent experiment at England's Newcastle University. A poster with a pair of eyes was placed above a canteen honesty box. "People taking a hot drink put almost three times as much money in the box with the eyes present as they did when the eyes were replaced by a poster of flowers." It goes without saying that people who'd had their fingers chopped off were five times less likely to pilfer the loose change. What Singer fails to appreciate is that once a society ceases to trust its people, it exempts them from any obligation to be trustworthy. As Charles Fried wrote more than fifty years ago (also on an issue of penology): "Unmonitored release affirms . . . the relations of trust between the convicted criminal and society which the criminal violated by his crime and which we should now be seeking to reestablish." This raises the question of how relations of trust could be reestablished in a "panoptical" society whose members had no other reason to obey the law than the fear of someone's eyes on them.

Such a fear provokes resistance. Or it should. Rooted in our repugnance to bodily violation, privacy can be viewed as resistance in its most primal form—one reason why, in cases where pacification is the goal of power, privacy is reduced as much as possible. All top-down "totalizing" institutions, including abusive households, thrive on the elimination of privacy. If they can overcome initial resistance, if the "inmate" can be made to feel that nothing is hers, not even herself, the result will be learned helplessness, "a state in which organisms almost become nonfunctional because of inability to regulate exchange with the environment." This is why I believe the issue of privacy is of such contemporary importance. It is not the Constitution that is being subverted by Big Brother so much as the will to resist, without which there never could have been a Constitution in the first place. If I'm willing to accept that the National Security Agency or the U.S. military has the ability to know and even to predict my movements throughout the day, then how much will I care about the CIA fomenting a coup in South America? If I'm willing to have my person virtually strip-searched in an airport, then how much will I be concerned about racial profiling in Arizona? Resistance, like charity, begins at home.

Privacy is not only a litmus test of the will to resist; it is also the petri dish in which resistance is able to grow—another reason why authoritarian governments fear it, as well as a reason why antiauthoritarians should fear belittling it. Writing about the French village of Le Chambon, in which a population of roughly five thousand people rescued an equivalent number of Jews, mostly children, literally under the eyes of the Gestapo, Philip Hallie singles out for special mention the *privacy* of the rescuers. "Now the French, especially in the villages, are a very private people, as the windows tightly shuttered at night suggest." The rescuers were so "discreet, as silent and as separate as possible regarding the refugees," that some of them did not discover that their next-door neighbors were also harboring Jews until after the war. The Gestapo could have arrested and tortured any one of them and learned little—because there was little to be learned.

Here a reader might object and say, "Yes, but this 'privacy' you're talking about would not have been an effective tool of resistance without an organized community behind it." I would go further than that. The privacy I'm talking about would not even have *existed* without an organized community behind it. In other words, what I say in the first sentence of this chapter about defending privacy by defending its opposites works for those opposites too. If you love privacy, you also have to love the social contract that ensures it.

•

When Alexis de Tocqueville wrote his reflections on American democracy in the late eighteenth century, he laid special emphasis on the dangers of unchecked individualism. He did not indict privacy per se, but he came close, noting that the tendency of "each member of the community to sever himself from the mass of his fellows and to draw apart with his family and his friends . . . saps the virtues of public life" and ultimately "attacks and destroys all others and is at length absorbed in downright selfishness."

At the same time, Tocqueville devoted a number of pages to the discussion of "American honor," which he found to be in marked contrast to the older, more aristocratic honor codes of Europe. Americans were less passionate about matters of personal honor, he found, preferring to think in terms of virtues like honorable business practices. Tocqueville attributed this development to the greater equality and social mobility of American society, concluding that "the dissimilarities and inequalities of men give rise to the notion of honor; that notion is weakened in proportion as these differences are obliterated." Almost in spite of himself, Tocqueville may have put his finger on yet another benefit of that "dangerous" form of individualism we call privacy.

I mean the beneficial liberation of democratic societies from the lurid violence that typifies honor cultures. To live with little or no privacy is to live entirely as a public persona, which is to say, to live and die on the basis of one's personal reputation. And anything you live and die by can quickly become something you kill by. One is not surprised to learn that the Nazis were preoccupied with notions of honor.

You needn't have lived in Germany during the Reich or in England during the War of the Roses or in the villages of India and Pakistan today to experience an honor culture at work. You need only visit a prison or a high school. The social systems of both are essentially those of honor-based cultures. Privacy is virtually nonexistent. Affiliation counts for much of one's identity, be it with the Aryan Brotherhood or the cheerleading squad. Reputation means everything; loss of face is not to be endured. Disrespect me and you're dead.

Most of us, I think, are glad not to live that way. And if so, we owe some of our thanks to privacy. But the relationship between privacy and honor may be more complex than it first appears. Yes, privacy frees us from the daily drama, the ghastly vendettas of an honor-based society; but like a serpent eating its tail, a disregard for personal honor can ultimately swallow our regard for privacy as well. It becomes "no big deal." At times I wonder if we are witnessing the emergence of a new American type, foreshadowed but not yet fully realized when Tocqueville was writing his observations: a type for whom a sense of honor has largely been replaced by a sense of humor, for whom indignity is seldom so intolerable as inconvenience, for whom the phrase *to die for* most likely refers to some kind of chocolate cake.

I suppose we could do worse. In 1833 the French Duchess of Berry, imprisoned for her royalist agitation, was found to be pregnant. She was a widow at the time, and republican sympathizers were quick to publicize her scandalous condition. This was regarded in royalist circles as an insufferable assault on the duchess's honor, exposing her "intimate life" to "the insulting commentaries of the multitude." Duels were fought on her behalf. In a scene straight out of a Woody Allen movie, a handful of royalist journalists challenged their republican counterparts to a "gigantic duello." We are fortunate to be done with that sort of thing, not least of all with the idea that pregnancy is an occasion for shame, or that a duchess has more honor to lose than a charwoman, or that any woman's honor requires a man to defend it. Even so, I could do with a bit of honor now and then. I could imagine worse ways of leaving this world than to have died in a duel over Tyler Clementi's rights to love whom he pleased and to be let alone.

7

IS PRIVACY A UNIVERSAL VALUE?

A SECOND CONTRARIAN ARGUMENT

> I'm Nobody! Who are you?
> Are you—Nobody—Too?
> —EMILY DICKINSON

Granted that privacy might be important to *us*, but what about *them*? If other cultures seem able to do without what we regard as a fundamental human need, then might our need be less fundamental than we think?

Privately disposed men and women may find themselves annoyed by these questions. Do I need to have the entire Family of Man in my bathtub to justify closing the door when I bathe? Universality can go to hell—just get these people out of here!

Others, including critics of privacy, are likely to have their own reasons for resisting any claim that smacks of the universal. By now most of us have figured out the Catch-22 that informs contemporary discussions of values. Only a universal value is worth fighting for—and there is no such thing as a universal value. Now that we've settled that, we can find a nice place for lunch.

As noted by the late Tony Judt, this kind of "aesthetic and moral relativism" often boils down to the crassest kind of political convenience: "if something is good for me it is not incumbent upon me to ascertain whether it is good for someone else—much less to impose it upon them." In some ways it is as convenient to deny that people of certain classes or cultures have an intrinsic need for privacy as it was for the conquistadors to deny that Native Americans had souls. Anthropologists in particular might be comforted by the thought of a culture "having no notion of privacy" and thus no conceivable objection to perfect strangers nosing about the huts.

Tribes like the Gebusi of New Guinea, who are said to "shun privacy" to the extent that they will avoid looking at photographs in which any single one of them is depicted alone, and the !Kung (formerly referred to as the Bushmen) of the African Kalahari are among the top-ranked poster children for promoting the idea of privacy as a relative, culturally specific value. "There is no privacy in a !Kung encampment," notes a typical source, "and the vast veld is not a cover." Another contends that "privacy is not something most !Kung deem very important." These statements distress me not only because I hold privacy dear but also because I have a particular fondness for the !Kung. Their own name for themselves roughly translates as the Harmless People. How much privacy would you even need among a people whose very name implies a willingness to let others alone?

At first glance the answer seems to be not much. The !Kung eat and sleep together in small, tightly knit bands, sometimes huddling together for warmth in the night. They are "trained from childhood to look sharply at things," to "register every person's footprints in their minds." Like people in privacy-rich cultures, they are known to have extramarital affairs—except that these affairs are known to every other person in the band. There is little point in the lovers saying, if the !Kung language even has words for saying, "Mind your own business." As Barrington Moore notes in his exhaustive cultural history of privacy, "it is hard to imagine any one person" among the !Kung or other subsistence peoples like them "demanding rights *against* society, since the main problem is to preserve forms of cooperation that are a matter of life and death for everybody."

Even so, concluding that the !Kung have no innate sense of privacy would strike me as a little like concluding that the Inuit have no sense of excessive heat. *Look at all the fur they wear!* Put an Inuit in Spain in the midafternoon and it will not take her long to discover what the shade of an olive tree is good for. Take a band of !Kung to a noisy cocktail party and at least one of them will find his way up to the roof (where I will be waiting for him with a cold beer and a single question: *Have you been followed?*). Louis Brandeis famously said that "the right to be let alone" was "the right most valued by civilized men." Perhaps that is because civilized men enjoy it more rarely than do their "uncivilized" brothers and sisters.

When a pregnant !Kung woman goes into labor she retreats to a solitary spot in the bush, thus depriving herself of assistance and subjecting herself to various potential inconveniences such as jackals and pythons. Apparently it is worth the risk (though I wonder if the presence of outside observers isn't a contributing factor). Staring among the !Kung is considered rudeness, as is pointing at another person. Open displays of physical affection between adults are confined to those of the same sex, and a !Kung "hug" is executed so "lightly" as to have been likened by one visitor to "being embraced by moths." (Are you still trying to picture the !Kung at that cocktail party?) The same visitor observes adults to be "slightly inhibited" about urinating in plain sight or gallivanting from one *werf* (fireside gathering) to another. I suppose we see what we want to see, but this sounds like an elegantly simple version of privacy to me.

Surely one of the factors inhibiting our appreciation of privacy's diverse manifestations is our own privacy's reliance on real estate and tort law. We buy, rent, and litigate our privacies; other peoples enshrine theirs in custom and taboo. To say nothing of living in environments where two steps away from an encampment puts one in a place of solitude, or of living in a culture where dance and trance do the same thing.

Though he has been challenged since, and though it would be altogether amazing if he hadn't been, psychologist Irwin Altman speculated in the mid-1970s that many cultures have developed ways of coping with "departures from some optimum level of interaction in either a 'too much' or 'too little' direction." The strategies and the optimum level vary from culture to culture, but the "selective control of access to the self" is a common feature. The Mehinacu Indians of central Brazil, for example, seem to dwell in a !Kung-like dearth of privacy; like the !Kung they live a communal life and know one another well enough to recognize a neighbor's footprints. Nevertheless, they maintain secret paths and clearings in the woods for "escape from others" and frown on the exposure of other people's misconduct and the asking of embarrassing questions. (Reportedly, they would rather lie than do either; understandably, they lie a lot.) The Pygmies of Zaire periodically rearrange their huts and shift the entrances to different sides of a hut when troublesome newcomers enter a village or when arguments arise. Thus they control "access to the self" in what Altman calls "a dialectic process." For inspired simplicity, though, it's hard to beat the Lapps of Northern Europe, who allow random visitors to enter their houses unchallenged, but deal with unwanted or tiresome guests by pretending to fall asleep during the visit.

Even animals, according to Alan Westin, evince a need for space and freedom from molestation that might correspond to the human need for privacy. He cites among other examples a die-off of some three hundred deer on an island off the coast of Maryland. Although the deer had about an acre apiece, adequate food, and no known infections, they were still too close for comfort. Of course no dedicated pet owner needs to be told that animals have needs and feelings similar to our own. A friend of ours recently received a late-night distress call from the young entrepreneur for whom she works; it seems his pedigreed dogs had gotten into his marijuana and were "Jonesing all over the living room!" More common, as well as more dignified, is the dog or cat who begins Brandeising under a couch or behind a book-shelf. The visiting nephews and nieces, stimulating at first, have carried their attentions a pat too far.

•

No doubt we should be cautious about jumping to easy con-clusions about universality—if only to avoid the kind of pre-sumptuous arrogance that is far more dangerous to privacy than any low-dose relativism. Fortunately, we needn't put on pith helmets to produce a culture that defies any simplistic notion of norms.

For over thirty years (from about 1952 to 1984) it was rou-tine practice in the Chicago police department to strip-search all female suspects brought into police stations, but only female suspects, each of whom was required according to department regulations to "lift her blouse or sweater and to unhook and lift her brassiere to allow a visual inspection of the breast area" and then to expose herself below the waist and "squat two or three times facing the detention aide and to bend over at the waist to permit visual inspection of the vaginal and anal area." This happened to thousands of women, some of whom had been accused of nothing more than traffic violations. In one case, two women who tried to resist the searches were essentially fisted and raped with a nightstick by female officers who threatened to invite their male colleagues to watch. Another woman who had failed to pay several parking tickets and made the mistake of telling her uniformed tormentors that she was a doctor was ordered to strip naked and expose herself to repeated examination and verbal abuse. While admitting that there had been excesses, the city of Chicago adamantly maintained throughout several ACLU-sponsored court challenges and appeals that its strip-search policy was "reasonable" and therefore constitutional. In 1984 the U.S. Court of Appeals for the Seventh Circuit disagreed. The practice continued, however, in at least one neighboring city till as late as 1990. Among women arrested in Calumet City, Illinois, no fewer than twenty-seven had been strip-searched (including manipulation of their breasts and digital penetration of their vaginas) by male officers.

Minus the blatant sexism of the Chicago policy (predicated on the argument that women are endowed with extra places to hide stuff), strip-searching has continued to be routine in a number of the nation's police departments, struck down by federal courts in some jurisdictions and upheld in others. Men and women accused of such heinous offenses as "riding a bicycle without an audible bell," eating a sandwich on the Washington, D.C., Metro, and the "false pretenses" of "entering a parking garage and immediately leaving because the cost was too high" have all been subjected to the practice. In *Florence v. Board of Chosen Freeholders* (2012), a case involving a man arrested and repeatedly strip-searched in 2005 for failure to pay a traffic ticket he had in fact paid (his wife produced the receipt at his arrest, but the police computer hadn't been updated), the United States Supreme Court upheld the constitutionality of blanket strip-searches by a vote of five to four.

Try to imagine any culture in any time or place in which such outrages as occurred in Chicago and Calumet City, and are now likely to occur with even more brazen impunity, would be regarded as anything other than outrages. Try it out on the poor !Kung, if you must. *Among the !Kung of the Kalahari Desert it is customary in cases of a woman making unusual maneuvers on forest trails for several of the band's senior matrons to surround the transgressor, order her to remove the* kaross *that !Kung women traditionally wear, and inspect her anus and vagina. If the woman is known to be a traditional healer, the inspection is performed with particular roughness and derision. No one objects, however, since Western notions of modesty, violation, and even such binary categories as yours and mine don't exist in this culture. In fact, the !Kung appear unable to distinguish between touching their own genitals and having them touched by others, which accounts for the exclamation mark generally written in front of their name.*

Credibility failing us here, I suppose we could try our fancy on Ostrogoths, australopithecines, or the ever-serviceable bonobos, but I doubt we would get any further. I doubt, in other words, that any hypothetical subject could be imagined as finding coercive physical inspections "reasonable" or even sufferable. In any case, we still lack an answer to the question with which we began. Here is mine.

What we call privacy is a particular, culture-specific variety of an *essential* (yes, you read right) human *resistance* to being used or interfered with. It manifests itself in such elementary functions as covering parts of the body, choosing one's confidants, and walking or turning away from people when they become annoying. The resistance is strongest in defense of the physical body, and most noticeable in societies both large enough to involve people in daily interactions with strangers and technically advanced enough to extend the influence of a few privileged individuals far beyond that of their fellows.

This elemental resistance is found in almost all known human societies and, in simpler form, among mammals, reptiles, and birds. It might even be found among some fish. It is not known to have played any part, however, in the sensibilities of city administrators in Chicago, Illinois, from 1952 to 1984, Chosen Freeholders in Burlington County, New Jersey, in 2005, and five Supreme Court justices in 2012. Anthropologists interested in studying this extraordinary aberration are advised to do so while it remains in living memory. Privacy being virtually unknown in these cultures, protocols for field research need not be overly scrupulous.

8

THE PRIVACY OF THE GODS
RELIGIOUS ROOTS OF A SECULAR RIGHT

"Men sholde nat knowe of Goddes pryvetee."
—CHAUCER, "THE MILLER'S TALE"

The association between privacy and the body is at least as old as myth, which is to say, possibly as primordial as the first person who tried to bathe alone. When I was a boy and fascinated by mythology, it seemed as if the rarest thing in all the ancient world was an uneventful bath. Acteon the hapless hunter surprised the Greek goddess Artemis as she was bathing, David spied on Bathsheba doing the same, and Archimedes cried his famous eureka as he stepped dripping from an overfilled tub, its spillage having led him serendipitously to the discovery of an object's displacement in water. But that was science not art, an old guy naked not a girl, and so I would meander back toward Artemis, vaguely aware of the Beach Boys singing on the radio and other kinds of goddesses bikini-clad and golden by the waves.

Approaching Artemis was no simple matter, though. She had not been amused when Acteon accidentally stumbled upon her bathing with her nymphs in the woods. He was not a voyeur, like King David or like Krishna when he stole the clothes of the bathing cowgirls, but that did not prevent her from changing him instantly into a stag, whereupon his own hounds tore him apart.

"No man shall see me, and live," says Yahweh, the god of the Israelites, seemingly no more disposed to exhibition than Artemis. When the descendants of Cain attempt to build a tower that will reach to the heavens, effectively dropping in unannounced on the divinity, finding themselves in the neighborhood and hoping he isn't doing anything important, Yahweh confounds their language, alienating them from one another in the act of shooing them from himself. When the men of Sodom press upon Lot's house in order "to know" his angelic visitors (in this case knowledge really is power), the angels strike them blind, and with such devastation as to afflict generations of future commentators. Were the curse less potent, the word *sodomite* might have come to denote any would-be violator of the Fourth Amendment.

What these stories suggest is a sense of privacy rooted in a conception of the divine, of what cannot be known except through revelation. The idea is found wherever myth and taboo are found, which is to say everywhere. The Hindu god Shiva sits in eternal meditation with his family on the inscrutable summit of Mount Kailash; though deigning to be visible, the Buddha meditates in no less inscrutable silence, his eyes closed to our gaze.

As with its counterpart among human beings, the privacy of the gods is as much a gesture of regard toward others as a jealous protection of their prerogatives. When a mortal bumps up against the divine, too much information can prove fatal. After the mortal Semele extracts a promise from her lover Zeus to grant her whatever her heart desires, she asks to behold him in his divine form; no sooner does he reveal himself than she bursts into flames. Yahweh and Moses arrive at a more congenial compromise when, after months of meeting in a cloud, the lawgiver makes a similar request. "Thou canst not see my face," Yahweh answers, "for there shall no man see me, and live. . . . I will put thee in a cleft of the rock, and will cover thee with my hand while I pass by, and I will take away mine hand, and thou shalt see my back parts." The fourteenth-century English mystic Julian of

Norwich warns against seeking to penetrate the mysteries of "our Lord's privy counsel," though elsewhere she describes her Lord as "so familiar and courteous." She implies that part of this courtesy is not showing her more than she can bear to see, not being *too* familiar.

It requires no great leap of the imagination to move from gods who demand their privacy to human beings who require it too, especially in those traditions that see humanity as descended from or made in the image of their gods. Of course, one of the reasons human beings require privacy is to commune with their secretive divinities. Native American vision quests and ancient Mediterranean mystery cults were all private affairs. Even works of charity ought to be performed out of the public eye, according to Jesus. "And your Father who sees in secret will reward you." In his view the purity of the deed and the relationship with the Father are both compromised if "posted."

One searches in vain for more than the vaguest suggestion that omniscient divinities might also respect the privacy of their creatures—but the hints are there. "Will you not look away from me for a while, let me alone until I swallow my own spittle?" asks a harried Job of his creator. The God of Genesis does at least leave Adam and Eve alone long enough to swallow forbidden fruit. He drops by the Garden of Eden unannounced, but apparently he is not hanging around every minute.

The implied analogy between divine-human privacy and the privacy among human beings is more evident. Myths about uncovering the bodies of gods—unbidden in the story of Acteon, permitted in the story of Moses—merge with stories of human beings presumptuously uncovering one another. Noah's son Ham is cursed for gazing on the uncovered body of his inebriated father. Those who might interpret this as a matter of sexual squeamishness have not read much of

Genesis, to say nothing of later Jewish writings extolling the efficaciousness of sex on the Sabbath. Hardly a prude, Chaucer's earthy miller speaks his line about "Goddes pryvetee" by way of explaining why he finds it best not to be overly curious about his wife's fidelity. If his own sexual needs are met, he looks no further. In other words, God must have his "pryvetee," and by extension so must the miller's wife. Suffice it to say, the miller has not been influenced by any Victorian "valorization" of privacy, much less deterred by any cozy !Kung practices that throw its importance into doubt. He lives in the fourteenth century and has never been to college.

My point here is to emphasize that our sense of privacy is rooted not only in embodiment, in the vulnerability we feel when naked and exposed to strangers, but also in our souls—by which I mean no more in this context than the nearly universal assumption that there is infinitely more to a human being, and to the universe she inhabits, than meets the eye. Even Marx and Trotsky found it necessary to speak of the "spiritual" needs of human beings. Apparently they saw this as no threat to their position as atheistic materialists. And for all we know, our sense of the soul also has its origins in the body, that wondrous mysterium out of which and into which things are continually appearing and disappearing— breath and food, babies and tears. Be that as it may, you cannot open up the back parts of privacy without a whiff of the body's pungent insistence and an odor of sanctity too.

•

Human awe in the face of the ultimate, be it conceived religiously or not, gives rise to the idea that human beings are ultimately equals—an idea with far-reaching implications for privacy, as we will see. It is no accident that the concept of human equality finds especially vivid expression in religions with an almighty, transcendent Other. In the presence of absolute majesty, the mere rear end of which evokes awe, paltry human distinctions of class, talent, and political clout mean little. One might as well compare the relative sizes of a gnat and a bumblebee to that of the planet Jupiter. On that scale, both are infinitesimally small.

This is what King David forgets in what may be the world's best-known story about taking a bath. From the exalted height of his royal palace, David spies Bathsheba bathing in her yard. From the same height he orders her into his bed, and then, when she becomes pregnant, orders her foreign-born husband, Uriah the Hittite, into the fatal front lines of a war. But the mighty are brought low when the prophet Nathan arrives, shaming David with a parable about a rich man who takes a poor man's only sheep. The metaphorical comparison of a wife to a sheep, with all the proprietary implications, ought to disturb us, but it takes nothing away from the import of Nathan's condemnation. David has used his power to expropriate the good things of his less powerful neighbors, including the joys of their private life, and he in turn will suffer expropriation. Thus said the Lord, and thus will say several of David's more illustrious descendants, one a famous rabbi and one an infamous Red, but both on the Hittite's side against the king.

9

NATIVITY
THE BIRTH OF AMERICAN PRIVACY

And she brought forth her firstborn son, and wrapped him
in swaddling clothes, and laid him in a manger, because
there was no room for them in the inn.

—THE GOSPEL OF LUKE

It would surprise many Americans to learn that the word
privacy never appears in the United States Constitution. It is
not mentioned in U.S. court cases for over a hundred years
after the Declaration of Independence (not until 1881) and is
not articulated as a right by the U.S. Supreme Court until
the twentieth century is well under way.

None of this means that privacy was absent from the lives
of early Americans or from the minds of those who framed
our blueprint for self-government. Presumably there were
delegates gathered in Philadelphia who got through the drea-
rier proceedings of the day by anticipating certain nocturnal
enjoyments that are never named in eighteenth-century English novels but of whose existence we can be fairly sure.

When privacy does appear as an issue in U.S. courts, it
finds its first doctrinal justifications in several key amend-
ments in the Bill of Rights, most notably in the Fourth, which
guarantees "the right of the people to be secure in their
persons, houses, papers, and effects, against unreasonable
searches and seizures," but also in the Third Amendment's
protection against the compulsory quartering of soldiers in
private homes and the Fifth Amendment's protection against
self-incrimination. These justifications may lead us to a second surprise.

Many of us think of privacy as an abstract principle that we apply to particular breaches of confidence, violations of trust, or infringements on our freedom—and to some extent, it is. Trace its judicial and legislative history, however, and you find privacy emerging not so much from the philosophical ether as from specific grievances. The Fourth Amendment, for example, was not deduced from ideals found in Plato or John Locke; it was based on the hateful memory of unreasonable searches and seizures at the hands of British troops.

There is a well-known story of Samuel Johnson making his case for the objective reality of the material world against the idealist epistemology of the philosopher-bishop George Berkeley by kicking a stone and declaring "I refute it thus." He hadn't refuted anything, but he did leave us an affecting image with which to think of privacy. We can refute the notion of privacy's abstraction by imagining a Redcoat's boot kicking in a colonist's door. Every time the gavel of an American judge has come down on the side of privacy, it has issued another retort to the splintering blow of that boot.

Which is not to say that we are close to any final, definitive understanding of what one historian calls "our most contested right." For one thing, the boot is electric now. Of three privacy cases heard by the Supreme Court in its 2011–2012 session, two had some connection to technology. One of these, *United States v. Jones,* in which the Court unanimously declared police use of a GPS device planted on a suspect's car without a search warrant to be in violation of his Fourth Amendment rights, may emerge as "the most important privacy case of the decade." Certainly it will not be the last privacy case of the decade. Nor does the Supreme Court have the last word. Privacy is not the exclusive provenance of jurists and legal scholars any more than words belong to lexicographers or apples to nutritionists. Privacy is a collective work in progress.

The same can be said for the liberty and justice we

affirm as the birthright of all Americans. Add privacy to make three, and you have what might be called the holy trinity of America's secular faith. The values are distinct yet interdependent enough to comprise a unified whole. Without liberty—that is to say, without the freedom to choose—privacy is merely a euphemism for loneliness. Without justice—that is to say, without the fullest realization of democracy—privacy is merely the privilege of a few, often little more than a cloak thrown over our naked inequalities.

But without a decent regard for privacy, the drive to achieve justice rushes us to the brink of totalitarianism. Without privacy, liberty becomes the license to pry, exploit, and oppress. Privacy is the missing word in the Pledge of Allegiance. Privacy is the chivalry of the citizen. Privacy is the modesty of the state.

•

No account of the origins of American privacy will fail to give prominent mention to Samuel D. Warren and Louis D. Brandeis's "The Right to Privacy," which appeared in an 1890 issue of the *Harvard Law Review*. It has been called "the most influential law review article of all [time]." According to one scholar, the article did "nothing less than add a chapter to our law." Some have suggested it might have been better to leave the chapter unwritten, either because it is a redundant statement of rights already safeguarded by the Constitution or because it muddled the law with ill-defined rights. "The Right to Privacy" has been likened to Athena springing full grown from the mind of Zeus; but some might find a more befitting allusion in the myth of Pandora's box.

The story goes that Warren and Brandeis wrote the article partly in reaction against newspaper reports of a private party hosted by the Warrens. This was in the callow years of yellow journalism, still a ways from the randy adolescence of photojournalism but with cameras newly able to "capture" events as they occurred. Neither Warren, of Boston Brahmin lineage, nor Brandeis, the son of Jewish immigrants, was much impressed with this dubious "evolution" of the press. That's not to say they were without journalistic instincts of their own; you could say they scooped the 2011 Murdoch phone-hacking scandal by more than a century.

"The press is overstepping in every direction the obvious bounds of propriety and decency," they wrote, in what today's tabloid press might have taken for a mission statement. "Gossip is no longer the resource of the idle and of the vicious, but has become a trade, which is pursued with industry as well as effrontery." To safeguard the "sacred precincts of private and domestic life," the law must be willing "to protect all persons, whatsoever their position or station, from having matters which they may properly prefer to keep private, made public against their will." Somewhat in the manner of Samson Agonistes, Warren and Brandeis were laying hold of two of the stoutest pillars in the Philistine temple: the free press and the free market. They seemed to have sensed their challenge to the latter, at least, in arguing that the right to privacy was more than a mere right of property, being rooted in the "inviolate personality" of the human being.

As upper-crust gentlemen offended by the presumptuous encroachments of the popular press, Warren and Brandeis are often portrayed as having addressed privacy from an elitist point of view. One commentator notes "a curious nineteenth-century quaintness about the grievance, an air of wounded gentility." For this reason, and because privacy has sometimes been characterized as an elitist preoccupation, it is almost as necessary to define elitism in a book of this kind as it is to define privacy itself. Fortunately, the chore won't take but a minute.

Elitism is a category of etiquette that permits disingenuous members of class-based societies to attack privilege while leaving the structures of privilege untouched. Think of it as *The Communist Manifesto* rewritten by Emily Post. Its typical usage can be illustrated by the following parable. Two billionaires get out of a limousine in front of Lincoln Center. On the way to their private box at the Metropolitan Opera, they pass a ragged, homeless derelict panhandling on the lower steps. A college professor who happens to be standing within earshot is asked by the younger colleague on his arm to offer something by way of social commentary on the obscene spectacle before them. The professor obliges by attacking the *elitism* . . . of opera. He may even go so far as to insist that the inchoate mutterings issuing from the derelict are the aesthetic equal of opera. To say otherwise would be elitist. One can see why elitism is such a popular term, providing a little something for everybody. The billionaires get to enjoy the opera with the satisfaction of having had its elite status authoritatively certified. The academics also get to enjoy the opera, albeit in cheaper seats, with the satisfaction of having proved they are not elitists. As for Napoleon in Rags, he gets the satisfaction of twenty-six cents in loose change and of knowing he's the new Puccini.

We can charge Warren and Brandeis with elitism, and with sentimentality and paternalism as well, but they managed to their lasting credit to define privacy in a language that was anything but elite. Writing for the dissent in *Olmstead v. United States* (1928), in which the Supreme Court ruled that wiretapping was not an invasion of privacy, Brandeis repeated a phrase he and Warren had used in their article nearly forty years before: "the right to be let alone." This was not an original phrase—they seem to have borrowed it from Michigan Supreme Court Justice Thomas Cooley—and no one ever called it elegant, but the man who shined Brandeis's shoes would have had no trouble grasping what he meant. On the day when Justice puts her boot to the backside of the class system once and for all, the words will be shining still.

•

Not everyone would date the right of privacy in America from Warren and Brandeis's article, nor does everyone see its best foundations in the Bill of Rights. Recent judges have located privacy rights in the due process clause of the Fourteenth Amendment. *Roe v. Wade* (1973), for example, determined that "freedom of personal choice in marriage and family life" was a due process liberty. One scholar contends that "the standard history of modern American privacy rights" should begin not with Brandeis and Warren's article, "but with *Boyd v. United States*, four years earlier." In *Boyd* the Supreme Court upheld a merchant's right to refuse to hand over documents in a civil forfeiture case. "It is not the breaking of his doors, and the rummaging of his drawers, that constitutes the essence of the offense," the Court wrote, "but it is the invasion of his indefeasible right to personal security, personal liberty and private property."

My candidate for the birth of American privacy is a relatively obscure court case that predates *Boyd* by five years and the Warren and Brandeis article by nine. It is the first American court case in which the word *privacy* appears, and it happens to pertain to the actual birth of a baby.

In 1880 a woman in rural Michigan named Alvira Roberts sued a doctor named John De May for having brought a young "unmarried" man named Scattergood, whom she also sued, into the room where she was giving birth. Dr. De May had asked Scattergood to help carry his gear to the Roberts household and then had taken him inside. Roberts claimed not to have known Scattergood's professional status until two weeks after the birth, when Dr. De May informed her husband that Scattergood "was neither [a] doctor nor a student," adding that "it shall not go any further, or nobody shall know a word or any more about it." She also testified that at the doctor's instructions the young man had held her hand during the labor, and that he had looked to where she was "exposed" and smiled. Roberts's husband and a local midwife were also in the house at the time, though neither seems to have been present at the birth.

The court ruled in favor of Roberts, stating that "[t]he plaintiff had a legal right to the privacy of her apartment at such a time." It was as if the unsaid word suddenly had to be spoken, because the game had changed. The Redcoats weren't kicking in doors now. They knocked and you let them in. They held your hand while you exposed yourself to their scrutiny. They smiled. Then they sent you the bill. Not this time, though. In a decision that would be affirmed by the Michigan Supreme Court the following year, the jury awarded Roberts $5,000 in damages, the full amount she had claimed.

This was a fair sum of money for the time, and it surely would have seemed so to the Robertses. They were poor. Even if the trial records did not include the floor plan of their sixteen-by-fourteen-foot cabin, we could infer their poverty by other details—not least of all by their pitiful standards of privacy. Apparently, had the young man been a doctor or a medical student, perhaps no more than a married man, his presumptuous attendance at Alvira Roberts's bedside, obtained without any thought for her consent, would not have been contested. The poverty of the patient was inferred by Dr. De May before he'd even met her. When he learned from the boy who'd come to fetch him that two other doctors had already refused to come, he "guessed the reason was that the pay wasn't very good."

Testimony at the trial did not agree on all points. According to the midwife, who remained at the house in spite of her having been passed over in favor of the doctor, the Robertses were aware from the start that Scattergood had no medical credentials. My hunch is that this information might possibly have been dropped or hinted at in some way (perhaps hypothesized aloud by the resentful midwife, which would explain why the doctor revealed the information as if for the first time to Roberts's husband after the birth), and that the Robertses either did not register it in the stress of the circumstances or else chose to forget it as something they dared not challenge at the time.

My hunch will hold water for anyone who has attended a loved one in a medical emergency or worked as an advocate for the aged, the poor, or the otherwise disadvantaged. Advocates in particular will understand the hostage mentality of marginalized patients dependent for their deliverance on an all-powerful professional. Asking such people if they'd have any objection to some optional waiver of their privacy rights is like having your daughter's kidnapper ask if you'd mind him using your restroom before he tells you the terms of her ransom. *Whatever you do, don't make him mad at us!* This would not have been an unfounded fear for Alvira Roberts. On two occasions during the time of her lying-in, Dr. De May considered staying home instead of going to attend her.

The predicament of Alvira Roberts reminds me of an exchange I had in the course of researching a magazine article. I had been assigned to write on "the right to die," another area of privacy in which the courts have yet to hear their last case. I went to interview a renowned palliative care doctor, an outspoken critic of Oregon's "Death with Dignity" law, and an author of several books on care for the dying. When

I arrived at the teaching hospital where he practiced, his nurse practitioner told me that I would need to be mindful of patient privacy when I followed the doctor on his rounds, as well as open to the possibility that some patients might not give the doctor permission for me to be present. Roughly speaking, I was to be cast in the role of a vetted Scattergood. Both the nurse and the doctor seemed taken aback when I informed them that I had no intention of following the doctor on his rounds. I explained myself with a simple rhetorical question, one not without relevance to the Roberts case: "How do you withhold permission from the man who doles out your pain medicine?"

Commentators on *De May v. Roberts* have not always seen the case as an unqualified victory for privacy, for women, or for Alvira Roberts. In an analysis both nuanced and sympathetic, Caroline Danielson writes: "Alvira Roberts won, but De May's position, not only as a legitimate presence within her private sphere, but also, ironically, as guarantor of her privacy, was consolidated." Anita L. Allen and Erin Mack have little use for the case, which in their eyes "is better viewed as a vindication of women's modesty" than of the right to privacy, and not much use either for Alvira Roberts as a legitimate complainant. "For, absent exceedingly strong female modesty and seclusion standards, it is difficult to explain why Mr. Scattergood and Dr. De May should have been liable at all," they write.

What the authors have difficulty seeing and what Danielson does see, though she chooses to relegate the observation to the fine print of an endnote, is nothing less than the central question of the case: Would any of this have happened had Alvira Roberts belonged to a different social class? If Alvira Roberts had been Mrs. Louis Brandeis, or for that matter, had she been Dr. Anita Allen or Dr. Erin Mack, would Dr. John De May have even *dreamed* of bringing "a jeweler and tinker of watches" into any room where she was giving birth? Scattergood would no more have entered that room than Alvira Roberts would have been admitted to a meeting of Skull and Bones, unless of course she was waiting the tables or had been persuaded to dance on one.

As for her husband, he was not even admitted to her bedside. Danielson says that "Scattergood is the cipher in the case," though if he is the cipher, Mr. Roberts is the flyspeck. He is almost invisible. Interestingly, given all the "gendered" baggage with which the case has been freighted, he did not join his wife in bringing suit. We are not sure if this was out of shyness, or indifference, or a respect for his wife and her dignity as a plaintiff that would have been as notable for his day as it apparently is for ours. What his wishes might have been at the time of the birth, we dare not so much as consider. But is it even remotely plausible that Alvira Roberts might have wished to hold the hand of the man with whom she'd conceived her child, notwithstanding the undoubted coarseness of such a fellow, and not to dispute that favors of this kind are best left to the discretion of trained medical men and licensed women of the bar?

In any case, I will always think of *De May v. Roberts* as the birth of American privacy, especially given its uncanny resemblance to a better-known nativity tale. Here in the light that permits no secrets is our put-upon Mary, and there in the shadows of obscurity is her Joseph, inconsequential as a donkey or an ox. Wise men from the East arrive to direct the labor; a young shepherd is instructed to grip the woman's hand. In the nimbus of eternity, choirs of feminist legal scholars proclaim the equivalent of a virgin birth. The squalor of the stable, its significance muted with each retelling, gradually fades from view.

10

THE PRIVACY OF THE POOR
ON INEQUALITY AND PRIVATE LIFE

He lives without privacy in a lidless room.
—SYLVIA PLATH

One of my favorite pieces of privacy lore, right up there with billionaire recluse Howard Hughes retaining a barber round the clock in case he should want a private haircut at an odd hour of the day, has to do with the Byzantine empress Theodora, at whose death in 548 CE her husband, Justinian, discovered she had been hiding a heretical bishop in her chambers for twelve years. Now *that's* privacy. You can bet that if Theodora took to bed in childbirth, none of her attending physicians (probably women, according to the practice of the barbaric Byzantines) would have brought in one of their litter bearers to hold her hand during contractions. Justinian being otherwise occupied, Theodora could always in a pinch have called on ex-patriarch Anthimus to come out from behind the drapes. But the call would have been hers to make.

"Privacy . . . asserts power, and power confers privacy," writes Bonnie S. McDougall, hitting the nail squarely on the head, though historians would add several qualifications. For one thing, privacy is not so easy to come by when you're being waited on hand and foot. "They cannot even find privacy on their privy!" Montaigne said of those whom "ambition" had rewarded. "Eavesdropping Zenobia accepted," William Trevor writes of a domestic servant in his novel *Death in Summer*, but "the investigation of private correspondence, and poking about in drawers, she preferred to believe did not occur"—perhaps because her husband has no scruples about doing either whenever their employers' backs are turned. The public obligations of prominently powerful people can also constrain their private lives. Theodora's emperor husband lived a life circumscribed by official duties and ceremonies, and though he might have had as much opportunity as she to hide heretical theologians in his chambers, he would have been at less liberty to enjoy their conversation.

Nevertheless, the powerful have usually found ways to set themselves apart. By late medieval times it had become customary for lords and high-ranking prelates to withdraw from their dining retainers and take meals in private. The egalitarian round table at which King Arthur feasted with his knights had given way to a more hierarchical system of seating, just as King Arthur himself had been superseded by a divinely anointed king. The custom of ships' captains dining in a private cabin is of long standing. Even on casual Fridays in the most unbuttoned modern office, a stranger can usually tell the top dogs from the pups by who has a door on his or her office and by how often the door is shut. To say nothing about the doors no pup will ever see. Compare the 1968 GM executive's salary at 66 times that of an auto worker to that of today's Walmart executive at 900 times that of his lowest paid employee and you enter a universe where even divinely anointed kings have the relative magnitude of asteroids.

With income disparity of that kind—with one in six Americans living in poverty as of 2010, according to the U.S. Census Bureau—the difference in privacy between rich and poor will also be magnified, in ways both obvious and subtle. Paul Fussell, author of *Class*, finds obvious examples in privacy fences and drives. "If you're not able to find some people's driveways at all, you are safe to infer that they're top-out-of-sight. It's only with the upper [as opposed to up-permost] class that driveways become visible and available for study. In general, we can say that there, the longer the drive the higher the class." More subtle correlations between class and privacy invite analysis, precedents for which are at least as old as Marx. Noting that the laborer becomes nothing but his labor, Marx goes on to catalog the aspects of private life that are denied him: "Time for education, for intellectual development, for the fulfilling of social functions and for social intercourse, for the free play of his body and mental activity, even the rest time of Sunday (and that in a country of Sabbatarians!)—moonshine!" We should not be misled by the masculine pronoun: at the time Marx was writing, more English workers (many of them women) were employed in domestic service than in all factories combined. It need hardly be said that domestic service does not leave one much, if any, time for the privacy of a domicile. Neither does working three jobs in order to pay rent.

Mention Marx and you have to mention class warfare; indeed, the mere mention of economic inequality prompts the accusation that you are trying to foment it. A recent political cartoon portrays President Obama driving a tank labeled "class warfare," a response to his meek suggestion that tax rates for the rich be returned to the lavishly favorable levels in place before the Bush tax cuts bumped lavish to obscene. It is a sign of the times when a centrist like Obama is accused of fomenting class war!

What such accusations ignore is the sub-rosa class warfare that goes on all the time. No foment required. Not infrequently privacy is the field of engagement. Top-down assaults are easy to identify in the routine police pat-downs of poor and minority citizens and in the surveillance and full body searches in prisons, where minorities are disproportionately incarcerated. At the same time as the Reagan administration was arguing that disclosing the names of campaign contributors who'd kicked in half a million dollars or more to the Presidential Transition Trust and the Presidential Transition Foundation would violate donors' privacy, the president was preparing to propose a massive computer data bank containing every recipient of federal welfare, a "strong deterrent to fraud and abuse." Meeting with stiff resistance from the ACLU and members of Congress, the National Recipient Information System did not float, but privacy historian Frederick S. Lane notes a "rapidly growing 'privacy divide' in American society" as a feature of the period. "People at the lower end of the economic scale or in need of help were forced to make their lives an open book, but for those with sufficient economic resources, privacy was a privilege that could more easily be maintained."

Violations of privacy can work up the class ladder as well as down. The only thing a rogue cop loves more than shaking down a Hispanic kid in a lowrider is getting his hands on a college professor in a Saab. (Jackpot if the college professor is black.) A pandering media voyeurism focused on the lives of the rich and famous, the use of noise to violate the peace of private dwellings, the forcible entry of those dwellings to assault and rob, the scorn leveled against any attempt on the part of one's perceived betters to seal themselves off from scrutiny (in a small town close to mine a retired professor's "snob hedge" has been roundly attacked in letters to the newspaper and in outlandish complaints by the town road crew) are all examples of bottom-up class war waged on the field of privacy. They are also examples of impotence, of the bull that misses the matador in the act of attacking his cape. More than one privacy expert has posited that privacy rubs against the grain of democratic sentiment; it would be more accurate to say that resentment of upper-class privacy is used as a sentimental distraction from the class system itself.

The tactic is exposed in all its ugly clarity whenever it is suggested that "economic factors such as poverty . . . make privacy less important" to the poor, as a seminal text on privacy asserts; that "such patients [in Egyptian clinics that serve the poor] may be less concerned with privacy" than patients from the middle classes, as one anthropological study puts it. Italian sociologist Chiara Saraceno notes that low-income apartments constructed in her country during the 1930s "usually did not have toilets and bathrooms, and often not even running water. This was the result of an image of the working-class family as different from bourgeois and middle-class families in terms of needs and values." That image persists whenever privacy is labeled as elitist, with all the attendant disingenuousness noted in the preceding chapter. Fresh fruits and vegetables, choice cuts of meats—elitist fare like that doesn't appeal to the underclass palate, and therefore we should have no qualms about eating it all ourselves.

•

If you have any doubt about the value of privacy for all classes, you need only consider people wretched enough to have none of it. The pilloried malefactor, the slave in the windowless slave cabin (or worse still, in the master's house), the human curiosity exhibited for popular amusement—like the unfortunate African "pygmy" Ota Benga, exhibited at the 1904 World's Fair and later at the Bronx Zoo (for a time he was caged with a chimpanzee) until he managed to shoot himself through the heart—bear witness to the totalitarian loneliness of living totally exposed. I use the word *totalitarian* in its fullest sense. Writing from personal experience, the Czech writer Milan Kundera speaks of the "old revolution-

ary utopia, whether fascist or communist: life without secrets, where public life and private life are one and the same."

To hold forth on the false dichotomy of public and private, a favorite trope among those with private offices in
which to write theoretical critiques of privacy, is like decon-
structing the "arbitrary" barrier between salt water and fresh.
In the end, all you have is salt. Anyone who fails to see that
needs to spend time with those under "correctional supervision," a category that now includes over six million Americans, more black men than were in slavery in 1850, and some
50,000 inmates consigned to the mock "privacy" of solitary
confinement.

Constitutional scholar Kenneth Karst notes that habeas
corpus and the tort against false imprisonment both rest
partly on the recognition that prison is a harmful place to
be. It is harmful because, among other things, it robs the
incarcerated of privacy and what Karst refers to as "the freedom of intimate association" with those they love. Prisoners
are routinely subjected to invasive inspections of their persons, a condition that extends even to those who have yet to
be convicted of crimes. In *Bell v. Wolfish* (1979), the Supreme
Court ruled that inmates awaiting trial were not exempt
from searches imposed on inmates convicted of crimes.

Noting what she calls "the dark side of patriarchy," which
"permits (and perhaps at some level has come to expect) the
abuse of men" even as it fosters the abuse of women, Nancy
Levit sums up her study on men in prison as follows: "In short,
female guards can view male prisoners in various stages of
undress, but male guards cannot view female prisoners similarly disrobed. Women in custody are afforded more privacy
than are men in custody." She sees such an approach as rein-
forcing "social stereotypes of men as tough, sexually aggressive, and impervious to pain"—perhaps not the most
rehabilitating message to send to a prison population.

Conspicuous in their resistance to routine strip searches are Muslim prisoners, whose modesty code also prohibits them from being naked in front of other men (and from conforming to male-con stereotypes such as hanging pinups in their cells or turning weaker young men into their "punks"). Some Muslim prisoners have been written up, sent to the hole, or beaten for resistance to strip searches. No doubt their religion, in addition to giving them a basis on which to resist, also gives their warders a pretext for further abuse, a pattern well established by U.S. interrogators in Iraq. It is ironic that such a reputedly patriarchal faith should acquaint its male adherents with the same paradox of modesty that women experience in both Muslim and secular cultures: One covers up to resist abuse and simultaneously incites abuse by the gesture. Tell her to wear a veil; then rip off the veil.

Prisons are an example of what sociologist Erving Goffman called "total institutions," such as military camps and monastic houses, which constrain privacy as a means of fostering greater control. Nursing homes are another. They are also examples of how vulnerable privacy becomes when poverty and ageism join hands. Though "patients' rooms are their de facto homes," where "one lives among the things that help support the narrative of one's life," they are often no more private than prison cells, with open doors the norm and possessions routinely rooted through by staff. Any apology for barging in is likelier to be made to an outside visitor than to the resident. Medical procedures are sometimes performed in open view; in one case a staff member told a researcher that a male resident might be resistant to bathing by females because his penis was so small. Privacy in the sense of decisional autonomy can also be close to nil.

It goes without saying that privacy in such places is largely linked to one's ability to pay. It also goes without saying that many of the staff in nursing-care facilities are as poor as, and possibly poorer than, the residents they care for. Every day they get to see their future—perhaps a future they'd feel lucky to have. Class war can happen in these settings too. In my experience, though, caretakers and those they care for are sometimes united in affecting solidarity, a water thicker than the blood of indifferent family relations.

I wouldn't want to overstate the positive. I used to hold a part-time job that involved visiting people in nursing homes. Once, after I'd announced my presence at the reception desk of a long-term care facility, an obliging staff member walked to one of the single-occupant restrooms near the desk, threw open the door without knocking, and shouted to the woman on the toilet: "Mabel, your minister's here!" This was hardly accurate; any minister deserving of the title would have been smashing the furniture by then.

•

Having a right of privacy without the opportunity to live a private life is like having a driver's license without a car. It's not as though the license is worthless; perhaps you might be able to rent a car someday. But in the course of your daily life, privacy becomes an abstraction, an entitlement in your otherwise empty wallet.

This is most obviously the case for those living in abject poverty or total institutions. Legal scholars commonly observe that privacy in the United States, rooted in Fourth Amendment protections against illegal search and seizure, is strongest in a citizen's home. The decision for *Lawrence v. Texas* (2003), in which the Supreme Court ruled that anti-sodomy laws are unconstitutional, begins by affirming, "Liberty protects the person from unwarranted government intrusions into a dwelling or other private places. In our tradition the State is not omnipresent in the home." As the judge in *Payton v. New York* (1980) noted, there is a "zone of privacy" in America that is nowhere "more clearly defined than when bounded by the unambiguous dimensions of a person's home." But when a person's home is itself ambiguous, the right to privacy becomes less clear.

This can be imposed in at least two ways. The first is to deny someone a home, or at least a home in which the occupant is able to feel at home. Again, we can draw upon Marx, who writes of the way in which a worker becomes alienated from his own living space by the threat of eviction, by something so basic as the disappearance of air, cleanliness, and light. "The dwelling full of light which Prometheus . . . indicates as one of the great gifts by which he has changed savages into men, ceases to exist for the worker." Or exists only in the blue light of the TV. If this sounds a tad too Dickensian, then consider the unemployed or "unemployable" worker sleeping under a bridge abutment. What do Fourth Amendment protections mean to him?

The second way is to work the worker to death, drawing him or her ever further from the zone of privacy called home. Daniel Solove cites several cases from the 1980s in which the Supreme Court ruled that "people only have limited expectations of privacy" in schools and the workplace. It follows that those expectations decrease as the workday and school year lengthen; it also follows that longer hours at work or school mean fewer hours of private life.

These decreased expectations occur across class lines. The unskilled worker may need to take on multiple jobs in order to stay financially afloat. Her skilled counterpart may need to make herself available to her employer even when she is at home if she hopes to keep her job. Apparently as disinclined to attend meetings as I am, Oscar Wilde quipped that the problem with socialism is that it takes up too many evenings. Increasingly, that has become the problem with capitalism too. Work starts at eight, but there's a special meeting tomorrow at seven, which you'll know about only if you check your office e-mail before going to bed at ten. "People who work for me should have phones in their bathrooms," said an American CEO quoted in a book published in 1992. The quotation feels almost quaint now. For one thing, the requirement goes without saying, and for another, the phone travels with you from room to room.

The electronic revolution that we fondly proclaim as having ushered in the post-industrial era has in fact returned many Americans, both those in the service sector and those in the information sector, to conditions reminiscent of the industrial revolution. (This is even more blatantly the case for workers employed in manufacturing jobs in places like China.) Marx's depictions of alienated wage slaves sound more relevant now than they did in the days when my father paid dues to his union. For that matter, industrial-era unions that fought for an eight-hour day were effectively demanding hours of employment comparable to those in the Middle Ages, when an English peasant is estimated to have worked between 1,440 and 2,300 hours a year, as opposed to the 3,150 to 3,650 hours worked by his mid-nineteenth-century descendant. Presumably the reader has a calculator with which to tally his or her own annual hours of work in order to determine where they fall historically. Best do it quick before the boss rings you on the cell.

Add to these considerations the well-established fact that women working full-time outside the home are still doing an estimated twenty-five to forty-five hours of domestic chores on top of their nominal forty-hour weeks. Standards of housekeeping, driven by the anxieties that are advertising's stock-in-trade, have more than kept pace with the invention of laborsaving devices. In this regard, as in so many others, the middle class is forever struggling to catch up—to the poor.

•

I would not be writing this book if I did not regard direct assaults on personal privacy to be a vital issue, but in some ways the indirect assaults are more formidable. In some ways, what we call privacy has become a shell game, one in which a show of superficial confidentiality hides grosser violations of the same. Even the direct assaults work this way. One goes to the pharmacy, for example, where privacy policies are prominently displayed and a virtual ritual is made out of protecting the privacy of the customer. Don't stand too close to the person handing in the prescription until it's your turn at the counter! There you will be instructed to sign an electronic screen authorizing a "full release of medical information to any party connected with billing," which in our global marketplace means any Delhi data clerk with minimal computer skills and even more minimal requirements for a livable wage. Back home you will sort through mail from medical researchers and philanthropic organizations with the uncanny ability to guess those medical conditions your doctor's office has assured you are strictly confidential.

Similarly, we engage in discussions about the intricacies of protecting our personal information even as we lose our birthright to a full personal life. A man is fleeced of his pension, his right of collective bargaining, his chances of retirement, his likelihood of leaving a small nest egg to his kids—but look, look, here's an article about the ever-looming dangers of identity theft! There's a thief on your back porch, says the robber at your front door, stepping into your living room while you go to check.

11

PRIVACY IS NOT PRIVATIZATION
A THIRD CONTRARIAN ARGUMENT

> After a while you learn that privacy is something you can
> sell, but you can't buy it back.　　　　—BOB DYLAN

Regardless of our politics, most of us assume that privacy is
wedded for life to institutions having the word *private* in
their names: to private enterprise most probably, to private
property without a doubt. Any arrangement more equitable
and social, especially in the form of socialism, we take to be
at odds with our desire to keep some things to ourselves.
Though I intend to question these assumptions, I admit that
I share them too.

In the hands of savvy politicians, they are easily turned
into fear. Any diversion from the market approach, and you
can kiss your privacy good-bye. At the same time as Gerald
Ford pledged to respect privacy more than his predecessor
Richard Nixon had done ("There will be no illegal tappings,
eavesdropping, bugging, or break-ins in my administration"), he warned that a national health care system would
entail a "vast medical information network" posing "all-out
hazards to traditional freedom." More recently, a Republican
congressman has described "Obamacare" as "an egregious
violation of patient-doctor confidentiality and business
privacy . . . like J. Edgar Hoover in a lab coat."

These are not fears that the left has taken great pains to
allay. Where the conservative sees big government as a threat
to privacy, the communitarian, the socialist, and the radical
feminist see the American preoccupation with privacy as
an obstacle to better government. Amitai Etzioni offers a

"communitarian critique" in his 1999 book *The Limits of Privacy*, identifying privacy's limits with "the common good." Socially progressive critics have pointed to cases like *Wisconsin v. Yoder* (1972), in which the Supreme Court upheld the right of Amish parents not to send their children to school past the eighth grade, and *DeShaney v. Winnebago County Department of Social Services* (1989), in which the Court refused to hold a state government accountable for having failed to remove a child from an abusive home, as examples of privacy rights gotten way out of hand.

Be the approach to privacy defensive or critical, the underlying assumption is the same: Privacy and the collective interest are at odds. But are they at odds because conflict is in the very nature of what each requires, or because we have construed privacy exclusively in the terms of a privatized economy?

In the Swedish model of social democracy, for example, certain nominally private matters are subject to a degree of transparency that many Americans would find distasteful. Birthday congratulations are routinely published in the newspaper with photographs of the celebrants' faces—not by their families, but by the state. The salary of every citizen is published annually in a book. Children are entitled to take their parents to court (*Ingrid v. Mommy*). Yet for all that, the Swedes have been observed as an intensely private people, valuing solitude, cherishing their retreats to rustic cabins deep in the forests or on the shores of the country's 96,000 lakes, and supporting an ombudsman (originally a Swedish word) to handle disputed boundaries between public and private information. The time-honored privacies of "the home, the boat, and the island" are guarded "jealously." The "boomerang kids" phenomenon of adult children returning home to live with their parents, widespread in Southern Europe and Japan, marked in the United States and

Great Britain, and no help to privacy anywhere, is virtually absent in Sweden. In a report issued prior to the 2010 elections, the country's Social Democrats called for the construction of 50,000 new housing units, of which 3,000 apartments would be devoted to students and 11,000 to young adults, an implicit acknowledgment of an individual's need for private space. Contrary to what many Americans regard as an unavoidable choice, especially for women, between parental responsibility and work outside the home, Sweden boasts one of the highest birthrates per woman in Europe and one of the highest levels of female employment in the world. A casual observer might wonder if the Swedes have subverted privacy or raised it to the sublime. At the least she will wonder if rigorously capitalist societies hold an exclusive patent on the value.

Some years ago, an exchange teacher from the People's Republic of China came to our house for dinner and expressed his amazement that such privacy-loving people as Americans so seldom walled in their yards. He nodded toward the back border of our lawn, beyond which lay nothing but an eighteen-acre hayfield where the only prying eyes belonged to a browsing moose. "In China we would have a wall there," he said.

Admittedly, only an idiot would hold up the People's Republic of China or any other communist state as a bastion of privacy rights. Especially in its Maoist phase, the Chinese government sought to penetrate every aspect of private life. Children were told that "the dearest people in the world," their parents, "cannot be compared with Chairman Mao and the Communist Party." Couples were admonished, "Personal love is not so important: therefore women should not claim too much of their husbands' energy." (The energy of wives was apparently inexhaustible.) As more than one historian has noted, a key difference between authoritarian states of the past and those of modern times is the refusal of the latter to be satisfied with mere obedience. Unlike Queen Elizabeth the First, who qualified her demand for *outward* religious conformity by saying she had "no desire to make windows into men's souls," a Joseph Stalin wants the window and the souls too. "Dominating society through Belief was Stalinism's original contribution" to state terrorism, notes historian Jonathan Glover, something we do well to remember whenever we're tempted to take liberal democracy or libertarian notions of privacy for granted.

At the same time, however, we would do well to ask if the privatization of hitherto public institutions—schools, the military, the postal service—a trend rampant in the United States and vigorously promoted abroad by the World Bank, has left us with more privacy or less. We would do well to ask if the capitalist economy and its obsessions with smart marketing and technological innovation cannot become as intrusive as any authoritarian state. When Czech Communist agents were shadowing dissident leader Václav Havel, they sat near him in cafés; they went so far as to gird themselves in towels and sit beside him in the sauna. They stopped short of entering his house, having already bugged that. Backward bolshevists that they were, they never thought of selling him a smartphone with some sly software as part of the package.

•

If we locate the right to privacy in the human sense of embodiment, we can question capitalism's relationship to privacy on the same basis. "Private property has made us so stupid and partial," Marx wrote, "that an object is only *ours* when we have it." That is to say, when we can sell it. It sometimes seems as if in the act of selling our labor we have sold our bodies into the bargain. They are valuable only to the extent that they can be turned into commodities; otherwise they are as worthless as the air we breathe. If your body's really yours, show us the receipts.

The paltry weight often given to the strip search in the nexus of Fourth Amendment protections is a prime example. If we were to read that police had ransacked a jewelry store without (or even with) a search warrant, we might think the act an unwarranted abuse of power, but if they were to search a customer's vagina with the "probable cause" of her having stolen a diamond watch—or of having purchased a few lines of cocaine from a drug-dealing jeweler—we would view the search as a matter of routine. In other words, the jeweler's possession of the watch trumps the innocent-until-proven-guilty customer's possession of her genitals. These assessments would make no sense whatsoever in a culture in which commoditization played no part.

In his essay "Commodities and the Politics of Value," Arjun Appadurai has noted "the tendency of all economies to expand the jurisdiction of commoditization and of all cultures to restrict it." The economy's jurisdiction has now come to include human organs and genetic material, which are "mined" and "harvested" like minerals and crops. "We used to think our fate is in the stars," says former Human Genome Project director James Watson. "Now we know, in large measure, our fate is in our genes." So is the potential for making a lot of money, along with a new frontier for privacy abuse. A 2001 survey by the American Management Association revealed that 30 percent of large and midsize companies solicited genetic information about employees; 7 percent used the information in hiring and promotion. Meanwhile biotech companies "have flooded the federal patent office with applications to patent newly discovered genes" even though the genes occur naturally. One bioethicist has likened this trend to "patenting the alphabet and charging people every time they speak."

Even when individuals manage to rise above a market mentality, they do not necessarily rise above the Market. In one especially disturbing instance, families whose children were victims of Canavan disease, a rare and fatal recessive disorder, donated their children's tissue samples for research in the hopes that better prenatal diagnostics and new treatments would spare other families the suffering they had known. Later they discovered that researchers at Miami Children's Hospital had patented the gene for Canavan and the hospital was charging royalty fees for diagnostic tests. In some cases, the same families whose donations had enabled the research were charged fees when they tested for the condition in other members of their households.

For scale of exploitation, few examples can match the story of Henrietta Lacks, a poor African American tobacco farmer, whose "immortal life" is recounted in a recent book by Rebecca Skloot. Prior to her death from cervical cancer in 1951, medical researchers at the "colored" ward of Johns Hopkins Hospital removed and cultured Lacks's cells without her knowledge or consent. Since then more than 50 million metric tons of cells grown from this original "harvest" have been used for medical research, including the development of the polio vaccine, in vitro fertilization, and cloning. Of the millions in profits generated by Lacks's unwitting donation, her family did not receive a penny. They did not even learn that her cells had been used until more than twenty years later, when they too became unwitting subjects of medical research.

In an effort to curtail such abuses, the state of Oregon passed the Genetic Privacy Act of 1995, which mandated "informed consent for the collection, analysis, and disclosure of DNA information" and the destruction of DNA samples once testing was completed. The most controversial provision of the law was its "property clause," stating that an "individual's genetic information is the property of the individual." Not surprisingly, the most vocal opposition to the property clause—in Oregon and in other states such as New Jersey and Maryland, which followed with genetic privacy statutes of their own—came from and on behalf of the biotechnical industry.

Sociologist Margaret Everett, who served on the Oregon Genetic Privacy Advisory Committee and whose son died as the result of a rare genetic disorder, opposed the property clause for different reasons. Though initially she had joined the committee with the aim of protecting the clause against legislative revision, noting that she felt "very 'proprietary' about my son's cells," she eventually came to feel that "the proponents of individual property rights were encouraging, perhaps unwittingly, the very commodification and objectification that I found so troubling." In other words, her son's cells were not saved from economic exploitation simply by giving her an exclusive patent to exploit them.

Everett's experience of wrestling with the property clause raises questions about how we construe privacy rights within the structures of a market economy. Even when we oppose the economic exploitation of our bodies, we find it difficult to do so in any way other than to turn them into salable property. To use Marx's words, we cannot think of something as ours unless we "have it." Is it possible that bodily integrity and personal privacy would find better fulfillment in a society where neither could be sold? Might our genetic material become most indisputably ours in a society that viewed its citizens—as the parents of the children with

Canavan disease surely viewed themselves—as stewards of the common wealth of humankind?

•

Imagining such a society and how it might shape privacy is a tentative exercise at best, especially given that no such society has ever existed. Still, like the socialist Terry Eagleton, I "cannot accept that this—the world we see groaning in agony around us—is the only way things could be." Nor can I accept that the privacy we know now is the best we might create.

I wonder, for example, how privacy would look in a society of greater economic equality. We spy when we perceive a threat, when we hope for an advantage, when we suspect someone has something we don't—inducements all magnified by gross inequality and cutthroat competition. Tony Judt reports that between 1983 and 2001 indices of "mistrustfulness increased markedly in the US, the UK, and Ireland—three countries in which the dogma of unregulated individual self-interest was most assiduously applied to public policy. In no other country was a comparable increase in mutual mistrust to be found."

I wonder, too, how privacy would look if the private sector was not so easily able to act as a law unto itself. The Privacy Act of 1974, to cite but one example, aimed to "curtail the expanding use of social security numbers by federal and local agencies and, by so doing, to eliminate the threat to individual privacy." The law had no application to the private sector, however, where social security numbers continue to be used (and abused) as identifiers. Suffice it to say, I also wonder how privacy would look in a society in which all sectors were under rigorous democratic scrutiny.

And I wonder how privacy would look in a society

committed to what one legal scholar calls "Brandeis's vision of unmooring the Fourth Amendment from fetishistic property protection." One of the cases to come before the 2011–2012 session of the Supreme Court, *Federal Aviation Administration v. Cooper*, had to do with whether an airline pilot whose HIV status was disclosed in violation of the Privacy Act of 1974 (and with the assistance of the Social Security Administration) had the right to recover damages beyond his out-of-pocket expenses, including damages for emotional distress. I believe Brandeis would have sided with Mr. Cooper, noting as he did in *Olmstead v. United States* (1928), that the "makers of our Constitution . . . recognized the significance of man's spiritual nature, of *his feelings* and of his intellect. They knew that only a part of the *pain,* pleasure and satisfactions of life are to be found in material things" [my emphasis]. As it turns out, Brandeis would have been dissenting from the majority opinion.

Along these lines I wonder how privacy would look in a society in which private life was not so thoroughly defined and so frequently degraded by consumerism. More than forty years ago economist Gary Becker observed that as people acquire an increasing number of consumer goods, the time they spend with each item decreases. The ultimate result, predicted his colleague Staffan Linder, would be a "leisure" that grew increasingly hectic as people tried to keep up with their multitudinous acquisitions. Linder's scenario hardly sounds conducive to intimate association, reflection, and creativity—all qualities that privacy is usually credited with protecting. In addition to corrupting leisure by cluttering up private space and time, our consumables frequently include gizmos for peering into the private lives of others, or for publicizing our own in the fond hope that somebody else will find our frenzy more interesting than we do.

Late-stage capitalism seems to thrive on this double-edged strategy of marketing both the disease and the cure. The same economy (and sometimes the same corporation) generates carcinogenic chemicals and chemotherapy, literacy-stunting software and software to address illiteracy, fatty snacks and diet pills, processed food and vitamin tablets, laborsaving devices and exercise machines, deafening audio speakers and noise-reducing headphones—as well as computer spyware and security systems, infrared cameras and lightproof shades, guns for home invasion and guns for home defense. We are sold the bit for drilling the peephole, and we are sold the plug to stopper it up. We are sold the notion that this amounts to a meaningful choice.

In contrast, I wonder how privacy would look if education and the arts were shared fully with all, if recreational participation was prized at least as much as spectator sport, if public service was required of every citizen. In other words, I wonder how privacy would look if private life was not a junk-strewn island of exile but a welcome oasis from a full engagement with public life.

I wonder how privacy might thrive if the media were less inclined to voyeurism, if the ethics of seasoned journalists took precedence over the profit motives of those who own the media. I am thinking in particular of a plan put forward by Raymond Williams whereby the public would own and manage the physical "plants" of the performing arts and news media, while the workers themselves, the artists and reporters, would control their own "product." Might the production be less likely to involve such outrages as hacking into the cell phone of a kidnapped girl and tormenting her parents with false hope that she's still alive—all to sell a few extra copies of a tabloid newspaper?

Looking beyond Great Britain (where the 2011 hacking

scandal occurred), I wonder how privacy would fare inside a less aggressive foreign policy, which is to say, one with a lesser need to impose economic influence abroad and secure borders at home against the inevitable blowback that comes from kicking in doors halfway around the globe. In 2008 two government employees told ABC News that National Security Agency surveillance of suspected terrorists had included the monitoring of private communications by American tourists, journalists, and aid workers with groups such as the Red Cross and Doctors Without Borders. The whistleblowers also claimed that NSA officials passed around recordings of American soldiers having intimate conversations with their lovers back home. Let's say that I wonder how privacy would sound if the pillow talk of a twenty-year-old Marine took place mostly in his own stateside bed.

Above all, I wonder how privacy might *feel* in a society in which private life did not amount to the privilege of a few. Imagine a society in which one's most private moments were graced by the certainty that everyone else was able to enjoy their own version of the same. Imagine a privacy that was *free*—not only of intrusion but also of guilt.

•

Although achieving such a society is ostensibly a left-wing project, it is hardly advanced by those on the left who dismiss privacy as a bourgeois value. Brushing your teeth is a bourgeois value too, as far as that goes. Merely in terms of tactics, few things could be more off-putting to potential allies than the smug assertion that their "precious privacy" is precious only in the pejorative sense of the word.

Then again, putting people off may be the point. As George Orwell observed: "In a prosperous country, above all in an imperialist country, left-wing politics are always partly humbug" because "the majority of left-wing politicians and publicists are people who earn their living by demanding something that they don't genuinely want." In other words, a Maoist-style putdown of privacy may turn out to be nothing more than another way of "carrying pictures of Chairman Mao," to use John Lennon's phrase, a way of ensuring that radical politics remain marginal enough to be safe.

The disingenuousness of the tactic becomes clear in the light of more militant lives. "Conforming to the habits of her life and Marx's," writes Paul Lafargue of the death of Jenny Marx, "all care was taken to avoid her funeral being made a public one and only a few close friends accompanied her to her last resting place." The widowed Marx would not have been a more authentic revolutionary by turning his wife's funeral into a circus, but there will always be a few clowns who say so.

12

WOMEN AND MEN
THE FEMINIST CRITIQUE OF PRIVACY

> This right of privacy is a right of men "to be let alone" to
> oppress women one at a time.
> —CATHERINE A. MACKINNON,
> *FEMINISM UNMODIFIED*

We can wonder all we want to about what kind of society
would best enable privacy to thrive, but women have good
historical reasons to wonder which of the proposed models
would also enable them to thrive. After the revolution, will
they still do all the wash?

Janna Malamud Smith points to "an odd paradox....
Women have inhabited the 'private realm' but lacked the benefits of privacy. Historically, women have worked to create
private space and leisure for men." She quotes Sophia Ripley,
writing in an 1841 issue of *The Dial*: "it seems an unknown, or
at least an unacknowledged fact, that in the spot where man
throws aside his heavy responsibilities, his couch of rest is
often prepared by his faithful wife, at the sacrifice of all her
quiet contemplation and leisure."

The "odd paradox" is an ancient one. In praising the Athenian way of life as practiced in the fifth century BCE, Pericles
notes: "Our public men have, besides politics, their private
affairs to attend to." To women he says: "Great will be your
glory in not falling short of your *natural* character; and
greatest will be hers who is least talked of among the men
whether for good or for bad" [emphasis added]. Apparently,
even a good reputation was a tad too much publicity for an
Athenian woman. And apparently, all of this is *natural*. The

German feminist Beate Rössler speaks of a historical alignment of female, private, and natural versus male, public,
and cultural. Along the same lines, Hannah Arendt noted
that for the ancient Greco-Roman world the home was the
domain, not only of women and slaves, but also of the natural
processes of birth and death—all things best hidden from
public view.

Add to these abuse, for which privacy has long served as a
cover. "Privacy is about keeping taboos in place," Kate Millett
writes. "It is a sword in men's hands," according to Catherine
A. MacKinnon, "presented as a shield in women's." Neither
writer is speaking exclusively of ancient times. It was not until
1991 that the English House of Lords declared that a man
could be tried for raping his wife. Even outside of a man's
castle, we find the dynamics of his dungeon at work. Feminists have pointed out how Clarence Thomas's claims that
his sexual conduct was private trumped Anita Hill's alle-
gations that her privacy had been violated by Thomas's sexual
harassment when she was in his employ. In other words,
gender determines whose privacy counts.

Given that imbalance, and the historical tendency to as-
sign privacy a female gender, some feminists have attacked
the very notion of a "public/private split." In their view,
sexual injustice is virtually hardwired into the liberal definition of privacy as a domain in which the state has no legitimate business. Feminism, says Catherine MacKinnon,
"had to explode the private." She goes on to explain: "Just as
pornography is legally protected as individual freedom of
expression—without questioning whose freedom and whose
expression and at whose expense—abstract privacy protects
abstract autonomy, without inquiring into whose freedom
of action is being sanctioned at whose expense." She has
gone so far as to criticize the invocation of privacy in *Roe v.*

Wade and subsequent cases dealing with abortion, which she sees as having more to do with guaranteeing women's sexual availability to men, presumed as given, than with protecting their reproductive rights. "Preclude the alternatives [to sexual exploitation], then call the sole remaining option 'her choice.'" MacKinnon hardly speaks for all or even most feminists, but she is often cited in feminist discussions of privacy, if only to mark one extreme of the discourse.

When I was a boy, some Halloween marauders chalked an anti-Semitic slur on the sidewalk in front of our family doctor's house, and I remember my father saying, "For all anybody knows, Dr. Reuben may be the reason those kids are even alive." I can't help thinking the same thing whenever someone takes Catherine MacKinnon to task. She has dedicated her career to waging kick-ass war against the oppression of women, and neither women nor men who love women can know to what extent they have been her beneficiaries. It is the scorched-earth nature of the war that troubles me. If patriarchy corrupts a value like privacy almost beyond redemption, then of what salvageable value is the discursive language of feminism itself?

MacKinnon's friend and fellow hell-raiser, the late Andrea Dworkin, was less extreme on this point. In a 1978 "interview" with herself she wrote that "a personal life can only be had in privacy. Once strangers intrude into it, it isn't personal anymore. It takes on the quality of a public drama. People follow you as if they were watching a play. You are the product, they are the consumers." Then, as if channeling Louis Brandeis, she went on to note: "I think that the press far exceeds its authentic right to know in pursuing the private lives of individuals, especially people like myself, who are neither public employees nor performers."

Dworkin doubtless agreed with MacKinnon on our

patriarchal construction of privacy, and in general so do I, but with reservations. For one thing, I am not so sure that what we call privacy is of masculine derivation. Our stumbling block here is not only that privacy has been assigned a gender but also that it's been co-opted by a profession. When we reduce privacy to a matter of jurisprudence, it automatically acquires the deep voice of bygone jurists.

Might the originator of what came to be recognized as the right to privacy have been a woman? Might the ideas of personal space and private parts have achieved their earliest expression in a mother mediating between the needs of an aggressive child and his meeker sibling? The first !Kung woman to walk into the bush to give birth may have advanced privacy as much as the first judge to have retired to his chambers to reflect on it. Absent the meddlesome and mythologized serpent, the temptation of Eve occurs within a private moment. "It is not good that the man should be alone," says the God of Genesis, but perhaps woman was the first to discover that it was sometimes good for her to be alone, or in select company. In a recent essay Ursula K. Le Guin writes: "The conversation of the modest is what holds ordinary people together." Modest conversation, she says, is "the opposite of advertisement," and, we might add, the opposite of the bellicose posturing and self-conscious preening of men at war or in rut.

Le Guin is careful to distance herself from "the womanly virtues assigned by the [male] hierarchs—silence, deference, obedience, passivity, timidity, modesty," and in this she puts her finger on another feminist objection to privacy: its associations with modesty in the narrow sense of bodily concealment and shame. Here too the point is well taken; here too we run the danger of missing a larger point. The idea of modesty as intrinsic to woman's "nature," or befitting some shameful peculiarity of female embodiment, or as morally incumbent on women given the erotic helplessness of men— all of this is a load of crap. But so is the smug refusal to appreciate the existential experience of women in a whole range of cultures and their need to guard themselves against gawking. It is equally smug to assert that courts have been no more than instruments of patriarchy when they have shown particular sympathy for female plaintiffs who felt their modesty violated. One does not achieve victory simply by declaring it but by assessing the battlefield as it exists. Do women plant tiny cameras under the rims of urinals in order to take pictures of men's genitals and post them on the Internet? Do girls make videos of themselves having intercourse with their boyfriends and then circulate them after (or even before) the relationship folds? Do women punish men by ripping off their clothes on the streets?

Admittedly, these outrages may be as much the result of as the reason for modesty, at least in theory, but a pregnant woman taking a bus to her third-shift job is not living in a theory. "The crux of the matter," says Beate Rössler, covering a multitude of sins, is "how discrimination against women can be eliminated in legal and social terms and how the different situations in which women live can be 'acknowledged' without consolidating these discriminations and different conditions."

A small step in that direction is to appreciate, and for men and women alike to emulate, the courage of female ancestors who refused to sacrifice either their right to bodily privacy or their right to adventure. One thinks of those women on the Oregon Trail who spread their skirts into curtains so that their female companions could relieve themselves unobserved. (The Bloomer style, with its narrower and shorter skirt, was frowned on by westering pioneers as

less suited to this purpose.) Or we might consider Abigail
Adams, who, though deathly afraid of sea voyages, under-
took the perilous transatlantic crossing to join her husband
John in Europe. She insisted on having the filthy ship cleaned
from top to bottom, instructed the inept cook in the proper
dressing of meat, and mastered enough of the ship's nautical
details to qualify her to take the helm if the need arose. Ac-
commodations below deck, however, were somewhat beyond
her control.

> Necessity has no law, but what should I have thought on
> shore to have layed myself down to sleep in common
> with a half dozen gentlemen. We have curtains it is
> true, and we only partly undress . . . but we have the
> satisfaction of falling in with a set of well-behaved,
> decent gentlemen.

It is a touching passage, not least of all for the modest way in
which she compliments her fellow passengers, neglecting to
remark and perhaps even to realize that if they were indeed
gentlemen it was partly her indomitable presence that made
them so.

•

If the domains of private and public have all too often been
assigned a gender, the analysis of that assignment has all too
often been befuddled by class. The stay-at-home woman was
always more of a middle-class ideal than a working-class
reality. Not only have proletarian women often worked outside the home, the conventions of blue-collar work often as-
sign these women jobs with greater public exposure—to say
nothing of greater opportunities for being harassed—than
those assigned to men. The waitress, the secretary, the ca-

shier, and the household domestic usually have more social interaction than the farmer, the stock clerk, the mechanic, and the logger—and hardly have better days to show for it.

Poor and working-class mothers have also been the public face of their households to a degree that mocks any notion of gendered privacy. The wage-earning women of my community would be highly amused to learn that they, any more or less than their great-grandmothers, were confined by virtue of their tender sex to the seclusion of private space. When something needs sorting out with the doctor, the banker, the social worker, the teacher, the town official, and—on some past occasions still within living memory— the revenuer, it is often the woman who takes care of business, sometimes with and sometimes without her copiously bearded and quasi-verbal mate blinking beside her like a galley slave hauled into the light.

All of this tends to confirm rather than subvert the indictment of patriarchy, but it hardly lends credence to the idea of privacy as "something that women possess in excess." I suspect that the class antagonisms that have bedeviled feminism for the last forty years, manifesting themselves in women candidates with antifeminist agendas and in visceral distrust of female politicians with women's best interests at heart, derive less from working-class women's resentment of their educated sisters' *public* roles than from envy of the greater flexibility professional women have to spend *private* time by themselves and with their children. The "new feminist" slogan put forward by Crystal Eastman early in the twentieth century—"Home for women too"—is still poignant and still new for those women who support the exquisite privacies of professional couples with their own underpaid caretaking and domestic toil.

Overemphasis on the historical feminization of the

private also carries the risk of underemphasizing the historical contributions of women to public life. To hear some historians speak of women's seclusion in nineteenth-century American society—"virtually hostages to their homes"—one might assume that the abolitionist and temperance movements were nothing more than stag parties with reformist agendas. When a group of clergymen presumed to advise members of the New York Female Reform Society (founded in 1834) to leave certain issues of social reform to men, its journal, the *Advocate*, begged to disagree, though *begged* is hardly the right word: "We allude to the tyranny exercised in the HOME department, where lordly man, 'clothed in a little brief authority,' rules his trembling subjects with a rod of iron . . . exalting in his fancied superiority. Instead of regarding his wife as a help-mate for him, an equal sharer in his joys and sorrows, he looks upon her as a useful article of furniture."

The key word is *equal*, of course, though its future was to remain shaky at best—not only in the forces arrayed against feminism, but within feminism itself. In *Women and the Common Life*, written shortly before he died, Christopher Lasch contended that when nineteenth-century feminism made a tactical shift from an emphasis on sexual equality to one of feminine moral superiority, it served to strengthen the cult of bourgeois domesticity and the encroachment of the "expert" upon the sphere of domestic life. "If a difference in sex involves superiority," wrote Elizabeth Cady Stanton, "then we claim it for women." If "the feminine element" had "asserted itself from the beginning," she maintained, then "governments of force and religions of damnation would have been modified long ago." Capital punishment and war would never have "emanated from the mother soul." These were compelling arguments for injecting the "mother soul" more fully into public life—I come close to echoing them in my speculation about privacy's origins—but they tended at the same time to ground women's "superiority" in the exercise of their domestic roles.

The issue of sexual "equality versus difference" continues to be hashed out among feminists. That should not disillusion us any more than the difficulties involved in defining privacy. Women are the equals of men, and require social and political equality to achieve their fullest human potential; they are also different from men, a difference confirmed by nothing so much as the existence of feminism itself. Still, one hopes for a synthesis. Of more practical use to humankind than a unified theory of physics would be a unified theory of feminism. I don't know if such a thing is possible; for all I know, it has already been achieved. What I do know for certain is this: whoever does achieve it or has achieved it must acknowledge that work of such importance cannot be undertaken without privacy.

13

WRITERS

THE EXPLOITATION OF PRIVACY

I have a morbid passion for personal privacy & a standing quarrel with the blundering publicities of the age.

—HENRY JAMES, IN A LETTER TO
WILLIAM DEAN HOWELLS

It was a woman writer, Virginia Woolf, who gave women their best-known battle cry for privacy when she published her 1929 book *A Room of One's Own*. "[A] woman must have money and a room of her own if she is to write fiction"—and if, many women would add, she is to accomplish much of anything else.

It seems that Harriet Beecher Stowe, author of *Uncle Tom's Cabin,* articulated the battle cry some years before Woolf: "If I am to write, I must have a room to myself, which shall be *my* room." Probably owing more to a shared predicament than a literary borrowing, the echo occurred at roughly the same time as Sigmund Freud mused on what it is that women really want. Woolf and Stowe could have set him straight.

Perhaps no movement for emancipation has been so influenced by the works of literary writers as feminism. That may have as much to do with the complexities of private and public experience common to both women and writers as with the witness of women writers themselves. Anyone who thinks hard about the private and public dimensions of her life may soon be thinking about the writer—and quite possibly about becoming one.

On the one hand, the writer occupies a zone of extraordinary privacy—not only in the conditions necessary to write but also and frequently in the ancient sense of privacy as a form of privation. Economist Adam Smith spoke of "that unprosperous race of men commonly called men of letters." Add to material privation the social privation that has been the motivation for more than a few men and women with a literary bent. Alfred Kazin attributes the accomplishments of some of America's most venerable writers—Emily Dickinson, Herman Melville, Walt Whitman, and Henry James—to their profound loneliness. But for every writer who seems to have been writing his or her way out of loneliness, there seems to have been at least two more who wouldn't have minded a bit more of it.

Virginia Woolf, for example, went so far as to propose, in 1933, the formation of a "Society for the Protection of Privacy," whose members would resolve "not to allow pictorial representations of themselves, to give no interviews or autographs, not to attend public dinners or public events, or to see unknown admirers." Later in the century Edmund Wilson made up a form letter stating that "Edmund Wilson regrets that it is impossible for him to" perform a long list of services often expected of writers, including "Autograph Books for Strangers" and "Supply Personal Information about Himself." It's clear from his list that Wilson counted among his no-can-dos spending too much time rubbing elbows with other writers.

In the manner of boys trying to scare themselves, a writer friend of mine and I occasionally amuse ourselves by suggesting that the other take up residence in a writer's colony, which in our hierarchy of horrors ranks even higher than a bed-and-breakfast or a shopping mall. Needless to say, we were both luridly interested in Flannery O'Connor's account of her time at Yaddo artists' colony: "You survive in this atmosphere by minding your own business and by having plenty of your own business to mind, and by not being afraid to be different from the rest of them." Ditto for any atmosphere.

On the other hand, the writer's private occupation depends a great deal on public recognition. The root of *publication,* after all, is *public.* If for no other reason than the means to continue writing, most writers desire to be published. The more obsessively private of them might write under a pseudonym, as George Orwell and Isak Dinesen did, or, if financially capable, forgo publication altogether, as J. D. Salinger eventually did. "There is a marvelous peace in not publishing," Salinger said in a 1974 interview with *The New York Times.* "It's peaceful. Still. Publishing is a terrible invasion of my privacy." Surely many a writer with sales figures less impressive than those for *The Catcher in the Rye* has envied Salinger's ability to be so "still."

But not all. What more of us envy, both writers and those who have wondered wistfully what it might be like to be one, is the successful writer's privilege of enjoying private and public to such an expansive degree and in such an array of combinations. A writer can be shockingly revealing in her private sphere of action and, at the same time, discreetly intimate with members of her public, each of whom she encounters individually in the reading of her work. In an age when writing as a profession was all but unknown, Michel de Montaigne described what he called "a pleasing fancy: many things that I would not care to tell to any individual man I tell to the public, and for knowledge of my most secret thoughts I refer my most loyal friends to a bookseller's stall." Those (like me) who ascribe people's disturbing self-disclosures on the Internet to the false sense of privacy afforded by being alone in a room with a computer would do well to remember Montaigne, alone in his no-tech tower in the sixteenth century and not averse to writing about the peculiarities of his bowels. The "pleasing fancy" of which he spoke is not new; it is merely more widely available.

Of the aspirations that lead people to create an online persona, perhaps two of the most common, corresponding respectively to the blog and the social networking site, are the desire to be a writer and the desire to experience celebrity. These are not the same aspiration, of course. Even the self-revealing Montaigne considered an itch for "reputation and glory" as one of humankind's "lunacies." The wish to be a writer may be based on saner reasons. The chance to work alone and unmolested while producing work of acknowledged public benefit is one of them. The desire to produce work that simultaneously belongs to all humankind and to you alone is another. Even in Soviet Russia, Maxim Gorky's novels were Maxim Gorky's, though I'm not sure how the royalty arrangements worked. In the private pursuit of her vocation, the writer's time is less strictly divided between company time and her own time, a division that grew increasingly rigid with the industrial revolution, when, not without resistance, capitalists began installing public clocks to replace the sun as the temporal regulator of the day.

In writing about the alienation from work that he saw as the hallmark of capitalist production, Marx held up the work of the artist as a notable exception. Luther's motto "every man a priest" might conceivably be adapted for some future social reformation as "every man and woman 'a writer.'" That is, every person with a public voice and "a room of one's own."

•

As a form of exploitive production, however, the writing life seems to have escaped Marx's closer scrutiny. Perhaps that was because it had not yet reached its full exploitive potential in his day. Zealous for their own privacy, writers have often mined their raw materials from the privacies of others. "Writers are always selling somebody out," wrote Joan Didion, and she was not writing from the viewpoint of a victim. Neither am I.

The writer's appropriation of other people's privacy can range from the relatively benign form taken by Henry James, who based the lives of his fictional characters on female companions, to the more merciless exposures of Hemingway's *A Moveable Feast*, which recounts F. Scott Fitzgerald's privately confessed anxieties about his penis size and his difficulties satisfying his wife, Zelda, in bed. What typifies most of these examples, including some I wincingly recall in my own work, is the lack of reciprocity that characterizes all abuses of power, be it the power of a voyeur, a parent, or a colonial army: I can do to you what you are unable to do to me. Fitzgerald could hold his own with a pen, true, but by the time Hemingway got around to pulling down his pants he'd already drunk himself into an early grave.

One of the more distressing stories of a writer's appropriation of another person's privacy has to do with the poet Robert Lowell's incorporation of his soon-to-be ex-wife Elizabeth Hardwick's letters into his 1973 collection of "confessional poetry," *The Dolphin*. Hardwick got wind of Lowell's intentions before the book was published, though he remained equivocal about whether he'd publish the book at all. His close friend Elizabeth Bishop tried to dissuade him. "I love you so much I can't bear to have you publish something that I regret and that you might live to regret too." In response to rumors of what Lowell's book would contain, W. H. Auden remarked to a mutual acquaintance that he would no longer speak to Lowell. (Hearing of the remark, Lowell cabled Auden: DEAR WYSTAN ASTOUNDED BY YOUR

INSULT TO ME.) After reading the poems in manuscript, Stanley Kunitz wrote to Lowell, "not as your judge—God Save me!—but as your friend," that he could "scarcely bear to read" some of the passages; they were "too cruel, too intimately cruel."

But along with these cautionary voices, Lowell had others of a more Mephistophelian bent, including that of his editor Frank Bidart, who assuaged Lowell's doubts by saying, "The only thing posterity will not forgive you for is a bad book." When *The Dolphin* finally appeared, Hardwick was forced to endure not only the embarrassing exposure of her private letters but also book reviews in which her character and that of her daughter were coolly submitted to analysis. "I never want to hear from you again," she wrote to Lowell. Too soon to speak for posterity or what it might or might not forgive, Adrienne Rich was still able to articulate the questions posterity will have to answer:

> [W]hat does one say about a poet who, having left his wife and daughter for another marriage, then titles a book with their names, and goes on to appropriate his ex-wife's letters written under the stress and pain of desertion, into a book of poems nominally addressed to the new wife? If this kind of question has nothing to do with art, we have come far from the best of the tradition Lowell would like to vindicate—or perhaps it cannot be vindicated.

If I linger over this episode it is because it has left me with lingering doubts as to how I might have counseled Lowell had I been his friend. My allegiances are entirely with Hardwick and always have been, but I know only too well how the claims of a book "that demands to be written" can eclipse the potential concerns of persons who, the writer tells himself, "probably won't read it anyway or mind much if they do." The writer is kidding himself. "Write about something else in the future," the mother of Richard Rodriguez wrote to him after he had published his first autobiographical essay. "Our family life is private. . . . Why do you need to tell the *gringos* about how 'divided' you feel from the family?" I can imagine my gringo mother saying the same.

These literary matters may seem remote from the experience of nonwriters, but they speak to more common negotiations of public and private life—especially when a broken relationship fragments a once solid circle of relatives and friends. What can one conscionably reveal to whom? What happens when "our" privacy splinters into your privacy and mine? Surely it is not so easily divvied up as the furniture. Even more significantly, and more than most of us want to admit, the Lowell-Hardwick story raises the inescapable question of how much making one's living comes down to living off somebody else, and whether there might be a better way.

•

Sometimes the shoe is on the other foot: the writer's private life becomes the subject to be exploited. Hardwick was a writer, for that matter. Lowell's lifetime friend Flannery O'Connor was devastated when a reporter chose to reveal that O'Connor had lupus. O'Connor saw this as having no relevance to her work and felt bitter at what she perceived as a betrayal. She did not say so in these terms, but it is tempting to reflect that the journalistic discretion afforded to a man and a president with polio (FDR) was too much to ask for an artist and a (single) woman with lupus.

What O'Connor was up against, and more than one writer has protested, is the increasing tendency to focus on the writer's biography as opposed to his or her work. The tendency is as old as Boswell's *Life of Johnson*, but it has grown to rank proportions in an age when the entertainment media have simultaneously upstaged the book and canonized the celebrity. Some would even say that a working writer in our day can survive only by becoming a celebrity. Never mind her sentences, does she have a website?

"I hate tampering with the precious lives of great writers," Nabokov said in protest, "and I hate Tom-peeping over the fence of those lives—I hate the vulgarity of 'human interest,' I hate the rustle of skirts and giggles in the corridors of time—and no biographer will ever catch a glimpse of my private life." That's a lot to hate, but Nabokov eventually consented to working with a biographer.

"It is my ambition to be, as a private individual, abolished and voided from history," William Faulkner wrote to Malcolm Cowley. In the same letter he says that he would like his epitaph to read: "He made the books, and he died." Harsh as they may sound at first, his words suggest the formula for a sustainable private and public life. It would depend on a society in which no person's work goes unacknowledged, and no person's privacy is violated as a cheap substitute for acknowledging his or her work. Do I really need someone to know my shoe size and my cholesterol count? Isn't what I desire most an appreciation of my work and some confirmation of its meaning?

In some ways literature makes a better argument for privacy than the life of any writer can, though it does so in a roundabout way. By its presentation of a well-drawn character or a distinctive poetic voice, literature suggests what Montaigne was surely trying to get across in his essays: that every life is interesting. His "Hey, look at me!" was also a "Hey, look at you!"

But doesn't that insight work against privacy, inviting us

to snoop into everyone's life for what Nabokov sneeringly calls "the vulgarity of 'human interest'"? Not necessarily. Many of the threats to our private lives, it seems to me, come from people who lack much in the way of a private life of their own. Who would take the time to hack into someone else's computer who had a well-tended garden, a circle of loving friends, and a shelf full of good books? We are under siege by the vacuous as much as by the vicious. Surely literature alone can't eliminate the oppressiveness of certain lives, but it can assert in cases of lesser alienation: "I am of interest and worth your time"—and by extension, "You also are of interest, and deserve better things to do with your time than peeping through keyholes, which is to say, than living on your knees."

14

LETTERS
PRIVATE THOUGHTS IN PUBLIC HANDS

Everybody reveals his own soul in his letters.
—DEMETRIUS OF PHALERON

If we find Lowell's appropriation of Hardwick's letters so egregious, it is partly because of the sacredness traditionally attached to letters. For almost as long as they have existed, letters have been regarded as the approximation of a human presence. When Saint Paul writes to the Corinthians, it is the next best thing to his being in Corinth. "I prefer that my letters should be just what my conversation would be if you and I were sitting in one another's company or taking walks together, spontaneous and easy," the Roman philosopher Seneca wrote to one of his correspondents. "And private," he might have added, as their face-to-face conversation would have been. Paul's epistles were a different matter.

Horace Walpole filled forty-eight volumes with letters he had always intended for publication, but we will never know how many volumes it would take to contain all the letters written for one pair of eyes alone. Many of these letters were destroyed, committed to the fire after reading or after death, as Thomas Jefferson did with all the letters he and his wife Martha had written to each other before she died. There is something extravagant about such a gesture, far more extravagant than burning a wad of cash. No less wonderful to my imagination than all the galaxies we will never know is the thought of all the millions of handwritten letters last seen curling in the flames. But the extravagance is matched by that of the personal letter itself, written not for the masses or for money, but because the singular recipient was worth the trouble. Dear Kathy . . . dear *you*.

A number of genre paintings—many of them produced by the same Dutch masters who celebrated the details of domestic life—show subjects, often young women, writing or reading letters. Part of the attraction for the observer is that we can only guess what the letters hold. We assume that in some cases they hold what one nineteenth-century woman called, in reference to her own love letters, "a part of my being." The subject is painted in a private room, but stands before us in a public one—a gallery, perhaps, or an art book published for thousands—but only she and the person who has sent or will receive the letter knows its contents. The letter in her hand evokes no less mystery than the halo of a medieval saint—more so, in that the halo has a known meaning, an aura as visible to the ox in his stall as to the curators of the gallery.

The comparison is not frivolous. In the Renaissance it was believed that kisses were a spiritual exchange, but "more then [*sic*] kisses," writes John Donne, "letters mingle Soules." (Interestingly, he writes the line in a verse letter "To Sir Henry Wotton," who in the service of King James confessed "a special appetite" for intercepting letters in order to acquire "the knowledge of the secretest practices out of the very packets of the Jesuits themselves.") Just as some retired to a private place to pray—the "closet" chamber enjoined upon the faithful in the King James version of the Sermon on the Mount—it would become customary to read love letters in a private place. "I cannot bear to open them in a crowd," writes one nineteenth-century woman of her lover's letters. It is "as if thy head were leaning against my breast," Nathaniel Hawthorne said of a letter received from Sophia Peabody, a thing "too sacred to be enjoyed save in privacy."

The physical sensations evoked by the material letter are no less important than its spiritual evocations—no less fundamental than our "privates" are to privacy. "The body *characterizes* everything it touches," writes Wendell Berry, and that includes "the body" of a letter, its pages marked with the smears and even the smell of the person who wrote it. "Pray write often as you can," nineteenth-century husband Lincoln Clark implores his wife Julia, "and when you write put on your open black dress and beautiful white under dress"—an affecting prototype of the stock phone-sex question "What are you wearing?" When Abigail Adams writes to her absent husband John of the longing she feels, one can sense her breath quicken under the bodice of propriety—just as it also does when she urges her husband and his fellow congressional delegates "to remember the ladies, and be more favorable to them than your ancestors."

Abigail wrote as freely as her times allowed, but it was more than convention that made her circumspect. The danger of interception, always a risk attaching to the letter, was especially acute in time of war. In the previous century, during another revolution, Cromwell's troops seized the personal letters of King Charles I after his defeat at the Battle of Naseby in 1645. Hoping for a propaganda coup, the Puritans published the letters under the title *The King's Cabinet Opened*, a sensational attack on royal prerogative, but perhaps even more an attack on the boundary between private and public life. In a subsequent tract of his own, the king would assert that "a civility from all men not wholly barbarous" would have acted against such exposure. Historian Cecile M. Jagodzinski writes that "the discussion of the king's private person became one step toward the commonplace that everyone, not just the king, had a private self." Everyone, apparently, but Monica Lewinsky.

If Jagodzinski is correct, then the discussion of Charles's

letters may also have been a step toward the legal protections afforded to the letter in English and American law. The 1710 Post Office Act, enacted by the British Parliament during the reign of Queen Anne, required every postal employee, at home and in the colonies, to take an oath swearing, "I will not wittingly, willingly, or knowingly open . . . or cause, produce, permit, or suffer to be opened . . . any Letter or Letters . . . which shall come into my Hands." That same year Alexander Hamilton persuaded all the colonies except Virginia to create a system of postal roads and uniform postal rates, significantly "the first cooperative action taken by a majority of the American Colonies." In 1792 Congress would act to prohibit any postal service employee from opening mail; in 1825, it would forbid any citizen from opening a letter in transit "to pry into another's business or secrets."

These milestones indicate how essential the founders considered a reliable—and private—exchange of letters to the common good. They also amount to the mundane facts of a rather wondrous process, especially if you conjure up the image of United States congressmen enacting their statutes in wigs and waistcoats so that Julia Clark might write her love letters in an "open black dress and beautiful white under dress."

•

If privacy means anything, it means that a personal letter needs no political justification. Political protection of the mail route is enough. Nevertheless, there are political benefits to the letter that more than justify its legal protection in a free society. Even a love letter or a letter to a friend can amount to a small political act. Abigail Adams's letters to her husband certainly do, and in no small way. Near the close of the 2006 film *The Lives of Others,* we see the disgraced East German spy steaming open letters in the nether regions of some Communist bureau. This is meant to be a demotion for him, though in terms of nipping dissent in the bud he is perhaps more strategically placed than when he was bugging people's apartments.

Like conversation, letters represent the first tentative steps from the radical conservatism of absolute solitude toward public engagement. "To be friends or lovers persons must be intimate to some degree with each other," writes legal scholar Charles Fried. "But intimacy is the sharing of information about one's actions, beliefs, or emotions which one does not share with all, and which one has the right not to share with anyone. By conferring this right, privacy creates the moral capital which we spend in friendship and love"—and sometimes in commitments that move beyond the circle of friends and lovers. In the case of letters, this can even include the decision to publish the correspondence— not only as a declaration of the ideas that have formed therein, but also as a kind of public declaration of the "intimate association" in which these ideas were formed. In their decision to publish their intimate correspondence (*Letters Between Two,* 1933), the Chinese writer Lu Xun and his lover Xu Guangping were performing "their equivalent of a marriage rite."

They were also expressing a change in their thinking that had developed over the course of the correspondence. In early letters they were inclined to see private matters as less important than public ones. They were left-leaning intellectuals, after all, and native speakers of a language in which the closest equivalent to the English word *private* carries unfavorable connotations. But as their correspondence continued, Lu Xun, the more ideological of the two, came to reject his earlier "elevation of the public over the private interest." For one thing, his wish to live with Xu Guangping became strong enough to overrule public opinion. As is so often the case when we use the words *public* and *private*, the interplay was complex: The couple came to value the private to the degree of making their love letters public, at which point the letters became less private! For all that, their correspondence could not have been less than revolutionary in its cultural context, whether published or not. Subtract letters and table talk from our political and cultural history, and you can have what's left.

Discreet correspondence enabled Lu Xun and Xu Guangping, as it has countless others, to grow their ideas in the incubator of mutual trust. What's more, it enabled them to develop their ideas in a zone of relative equality. Lu Xun was older and more educated than his lover—at one point he had been her teacher—but one advantage a letter has over face-to-face conversation is that the communicators have to wait their turns. The man who never shuts up has to listen; the woman who can never manage to get a word in edgewise speaks. And the voice of public rectitude, ever loud and abrasive in its censures, has to speak in its indoor voice. One of the more remarkable things that Karen Lystra notes in her study of nineteenth-century love letters is the way in which "men's emotional expression," subject to "constant control" in the public life of the time, "fairly exploded with feeling, manifesting as much emotional intensity and range as nineteenth-century women" when they sat down to write letters.

Obviously it would be silly to claim that the tentative zone of equality created by an exchange of letters rights every imbalance. We do not banish class distinctions with a first-class stamp. In one nineteenth-century guidebook for writing letters, a Mrs. Eliza Farrar advises young women to be "natural" when they write to men—but only if they are "wellbred." This qualification is moot to the degree that an "ill-bred" girl of the time might not have been able to read and write at all. From that perspective, discussing an illiterate person's right to privacy is like discussing a blind person's right to watch films. I say this not to disparage the illiterate or the blind, but merely to point out yet again how shallow it can be to discuss privacy rights for people who have been denied the full blessings of their society and civilization.

•

Sending a letter is an act of trust on several levels. One trusts the recipient, as Elizabeth Hardwick did to her regret. One trusts a scribe, if one is compelled to use a scribe, though in that case privacy has already suffered a breach. "If you dictate verbatim, then it is good-bye to your privacy," Erasmus warned.

Furthermore, one entrusts a letter to an unknown number of strangers into whose hands it might fall, either by accident or by inheritance. Every letter writer—indeed, every person who values his or her privacy—is more or less dependent, to quote the doomed Blanche DuBois, "on the kindness of strangers." Given that strangers are not always kind, many a correspondent has opted to commit the letters of his or her intimates to the paper shredder or the fire.

Not least of all, the letter writer is obliged to trust the agents through whom the letter is conveyed. The most private letter imaginable amounts to a display copy of the social contract. Perhaps that explains why we sometimes associate the workings of American government, for better and for worse, with the postal service. I grew up hearing the disparaging remark that anyone who thinks socialism is a good idea needs to visit a post office—a recommendation that seems to have backfired rather badly in my case. Living most of my adult life in small New England towns with eminently reliable post offices has not made me an enthusiastic cheerleader for the market approach. A world managed by mail carriers, park rangers, and public librarians has never looked like an ugly world to me.

In terms of this last level of trust, the adoption of e-mail as our primary means of epistolary communication has to rank as a watershed in the history of our democracy. I would not rank it so high in political importance as the degradation of the word *friend*, but it comes close, and the two are obviously related. Granted, the sacrifice of privacy for speed and convenience is nothing new. As long ago as 1846, a Philadelphia newspaper praised the telegraph, which also offered speed at the price of privacy, by noting that "markets will no longer be dependent on our snail paced mails."

Of far more significance is the way in which e-mail represents a simultaneous rejection of *both* privacy *and* public institutions, no big surprise to anyone conscious of their interdependence. This too is as old as the telegraph, though the current magnitude of the rejection feels unprecedented. The private corporation, not the public servant, is now entrusted with our correspondence and is not overly fastidious about breaking the seal. Whether or not Mr. Clark's wife chooses to put on her open black dress when she replies to his e-mail, he is sure to see an ad for one as soon as he hits "send." He will also see an ad inviting him to shop for a new Mrs. Clark.

15

LEFT TO OUR DEVICES

TECHNOLOGY AND PRIVACY

> Machinery is adapted to the weak human being, in order
> to turn the weak human being into a machine.
> —KARL MARX, *ECONOMIC AND*
> *PHILOSOPHICAL MANUSCRIPTS*

It makes sense that technology has played a major role in privacy's story. The tools we develop extend our influence over the material world, and frequently over our less-equipped neighbors. If privacy is the right to be let alone, technology is our ever-expanding ability to let nothing alone. You have your arm, but I have my arm plus this nifty stick for lifting up your loincloth.

Or maybe what I have is a camera with a telephoto lens. Louis-Jacques Daguerre's 1839 invention of the photograph would have far-reaching effects on privacy. At first the process of making a daguerreotype was a time-consuming affair, its cumbersome execution a virtual guarantee of the subject's consent. You sat for your photograph, which meant you were "standing for" the procedure. But faster exposure times, the advent of negatives (which allowed for multiple copies), and the halftone process (which allowed photographs to be published in newspapers) changed that dynamic. Some of the earliest U.S. court cases dealing with privacy had to do with individuals contesting the use of their photographs in news stories and in advertisements.

The transmission of Samuel B. Morse's first telegram in 1844 also led to privacy concerns. Messages could be read by third parties, and they could be stored. These features foreshadowed the computer age, as did the willingness to sacrifice privacy for speed and the reluctance of the U.S. government to take any regulatory action that might involve nationalizing an industry. Henry Clay urged the Congress to do just that in 1844, warning that with the telegraph in private hands, "they will be able to monopolize intelligence and perform the greatest operations in commerce and other departments of business." Today he would be branded as a socialist; in his own day he was merely a prophet.

By anyone's estimation no invention has posed greater challenges to privacy than the computer. The dangers have been well documented and exhaustively discussed; they will continue to be discussed as long as the pace of technical development continues at its present rate. Although few things date a book like an author's attempt to keep abreast of digital wonders—something that might also be said for civilizations—I will venture to mention Apple's latest (as of this writing) iPhone, the 4S, over four million units of which were sold a mere three days after its release in October of 2011. One of its more notable features is Siri, a language-processing "personal assistant" that originated in the same Pentagon research agency that developed predator drones. Siri enables you to use the Internet without keystrokes, just as Verizon's new smartphone software allows people to purchase products they see on television by depressing a single button on their device. Convenience becomes ever more exquisite, but at a price. As writer Sue Halpern wonders in a recent essay, "Putting aside the issue of whether going from seeing to wanting to buying with only the slightest movement of a single finger advances the human condition, or whether the person in the next cubicle really cares how stressed you are . . . should we assume that all this personal information being generated and collected won't be used against us by insurers, or employers, or lawyers, or marketers, or the government?"

Of course we know we can assume no such thing, but even if we *could*, our information would still be vulnerable to freelance hacking. Sony, Citibank, Intel, Cisco, Google, and the Department of Veterans Affairs have all reported intrusions on their "secure" computer systems, not to mention the U.S. government's 2010 embarrassment when WikiLeaks began posting some of the 251,287 secret diplomatic cables it had managed to access. Security expert Ron Ritchey told *Atlantic* reporter James Fallows that he has yet to examine a corporation or government agency in which he has not found "some level of intrusion." And if this is true for companies able to afford the services of Mr. Ritchey, how much more might it be true for the rest of us?

Whenever I hear of the latest hacking scandal, I recall something Wendell Berry wrote some years ago in regard to the disasters of Chernobyl and the *Exxon Valdez*. Nature, he said, was sending us a message: "If you put the fates of whole communities or cities or regions or ecosystems at risk in single ships or factories or power plants"—and, one wants to add, digital systems—"then I will furnish the drunk or the fool or the imbecile who will make the necessary small mistake." Or the computer hacker who makes no mistakes.

Privacy concerns can only be magnified, or perhaps become utterly moot, as we move toward "Singularity," the ultimate synthesis of human and machine. To say there is nothing good to be gained from this area of research is tantamount to telling everyone with a pacemaker to drop dead. But there's a difference between repair and enhancement, and enhancement may be where the money is. In his 2011 book *World Wide Mind*, Michael Chorost looks forward to a future in which, thanks to a neural implant similar to the one that restored his hearing, the Internet "would become seamlessly part of us, as natural and simple to use as our own hands"—or possibly as the hands of a marionette. That the "World Wide Mind" might be controlled by the same people currently ruling the whole wide world does not seem to trouble him.

•

The history of privacy and digital technology is ironic in at least two respects. First, it is ironic that the inventions threatening our privacy were conceived in privacy, enhancing in turn the privacy of those who profited from them. The story of Apple Computer begins with two friends named Steve Jobs and Steve Wozniak exercising their "freedom of intimate association" at meetings of the esoteric Homebrew Computer Club in Menlo Park, California. As dramatized in the movie *The Social Network*, Mark Zuckerberg's brainchild Facebook—which at the time of the movie's 2010 release claimed 500 million active users—was conceived in the exclusive sanctum of a Harvard dorm. Having turned private inspirations into private fortunes ($8.3 billion in the case of Jobs, roughly twice that for Zuckerberg), our digital moguls decree to the masses assembled beneath their palace balconies that the age of privacy is at an end. I suppose the idea that a man's home is his castle must seem quaint to a man whose castle is only one of several homes.

The second irony is perhaps even more striking than the first. The inventions that become threats to our privacy were in fact pitched to our desire for privacy. According to cultural theorist Slavoj Žižek, "What increasingly emerges as the central human right in late-capitalist society is *the right not to be harassed*, which is a right to remain at a safe distance from others." To that we might add that the technological innovations of late-capitalist society often have amounted to a bait-and-switch approach to that right.

A video player, for example, would enable us to watch movies at home, far from the madding crowd. At the same time, movie rentals added additional data to our "information profiles." Congress passed the Video Privacy Protection Act of 1988 after reporters attempted to learn what movies Supreme Court Justice nominee Robert Bork had rented prior to his nomination. The eventual option of downloading movies and music from closely monitored websites makes the legislation seem as obsolete as Bork's old VCR.

Of far greater moment, the personal computer would spare our fingers contact with the germy keyboards of public libraries—as electronic reading devices would later give us antiseptic and completely personalized libraries accessible at a touch. But they would also make us increasingly identifiable, and our identities more subject to capture. With the seizure of a hard drive, an individual's "entire life is essentially an open book"—and a pocket-size book at that.

Devices in hand, we could now shop online, as opposed to waiting in lines with the plebeian department store set. The obliging store clerk was replaced by the even more obliging Internet search engine, so much smarter than the clerk because it knew everything we wanted and what everyone in our demographic wanted too. Our wish was its command—or was its command our wish?

Also in the interests of keeping our hands clean and our business private, we bought digital cameras, which eliminated the middleman photo developer—no more drugstore cashiers ogling our honeymoon shots. And the beauty of this was that we could post the pictures online, where everybody could look at them, or keep them "private" on our cell phones, where only hackers could look at them.

Likewise, a cell phone would eliminate the need for and lead to the virtual disappearance of the disgusting public telephone. If not quite our oyster, the world could at least be our phone booth—though it would be revealed at the close of 2011, to the great shock of those who hadn't already figured out the game, that no fewer than 140 million cell phones were equipped with Carrier IQ software, allowing service providers to log keystrokes, track user location, and intercept text messages. No doubt what I am about to say will get me called a dinosaur—supposedly an insult, though dinosaurs ruled the world for 160 million years and sheep never once—but I have trouble perceiving the evolutionary arc in going from a twenty-five-cent phone call made with complete anonymity and some semblance of a purpose to "unlimited free minutes" of compulsive blather purchased with the disclosure of one's Social Security number and minute-by-minute whereabouts, plus a monthly fee equivalent to the cost of an intimate dinner for two with nothing vibrating against your shirt pocket but your smitten dinosaur heart.

Even so impersonal and nondomestic a device as a GPS promised to be yet another magic wand of private seclusion and personal choice. No more asking your uncle to draw you maps, no more rolling down your tinted window to engage in ungrammatical repartee with rustic gas station attendants. No more late nights spent tailing a suspect either; police can now plant a GPS on your car, as they did to Antoine Jones in the nation's capital. Since the Supreme Court has proved a bit persnickety on that point (in *United States v. Jones*, 2012), police might try your car's OnStar system to make sure you're "okay," or perhaps one of Ford's new cloud-connected cars, which "collect data about one's driving habits so that car owners can share that data with friends," including the officers who "friend" you, legs spread, hands against the roof of your car.

It is almost as if, in attempting to hide from our neighbors, we put ourselves more at the mercy of opportunistic strangers. Offered our own digital caves, we discovered them to be glass houses. Surely this is a question future historians will ask of our era, assuming extinction does not come sooner for human beings than it did for dinosaurs: Was privacy seized from our hands, like candy from a baby, or were we handed privacy, like candy *to* a baby, until we choked on it?

•

Given the staggering impact of digital technology on privacy rights, I suspect some will fault me with paying too little attention to it in this book. Yes, I'm paying some attention to it here, but this is likely to be deemed too little and too late.

My lack of expertise and even greater lack of interest in gadgetry aside, I have not paid extravagant attention to digital technology because I have never seen it as more than a secondary privacy issue. In fact, I think that a preoccupation with devices distracts us from the major issues—in the same way as social networking sites can distract people from their lives.

Technology is not the problem so much as the almost supernatural agency we have ascribed to technology, and to the market that distributes it. The technology that promised to make us masters of our fate has instead become our fate, the omniscient divinity of a new religion, and a decidedly fundamentalist religion at that. Those who attack digital technology as the devil incarnate wind up playing into the same mythology as those who laud it as the greatest miracle since the Big Bang. Both assume that Steve Jobs actually achieved his stated goal of putting "a ding in the universe." (I assume he was not referring to the dings made in the sidewalk by those Chinese assemblers of Apple products who kept jumping to their deaths until mesh was installed on the sweatshop windows.)

The mythology is nothing new. It is merely the latest symbiosis of fatalism and addiction, a pathology as old as civilization itself, or at least as old as the first sad honky-tonk song. We embrace our addictions as a respite from implacable fate, and we believe all the more strongly in implacable fate because we feel powerless in the grip of our addictions. Like gods demanding the sacrifice of a beautiful virgin, the future demands that every high school student have all his or her classroom texts on a Kindle. So if you don't want your kids to wind up working as golf caddies for Chinese entrepreneurs, you better pay out. And if privacy needs to be part of the deal, you'd best heave that into the volcano too. Even dissenters are careful to avoid blasphemy: Perhaps you have noticed the obligatory genuflections performed by anyone with the temerity to question our digital destiny. They swear they love their iPods and wouldn't be without them for a minute. "Don't get me wrong," they'll say, in a manner uncannily evocative of "Don't strike me dead."

A second problem, no less tenacious than the first, and very much related to the first, is how technology operates within the context of global capitalism—which we also invest with supernatural agency, market forces being our version of the will of the gods. That artificial intelligence might be subjected to human intelligence with an eye to the common good and the preservation of individual rights is nothing less than heresy. Even the roughly egalitarian principle of net neutrality is frowned upon and periodically attacked as an obstacle to innovation, our preferred term for guaranteeing that the race will always be to the swift.

Comparing the clunky national industries of the communist state he helped to overthrow with their free-market counterparts in the West, Václav Havel told an interviewer in 1986: "I would even say that, from a certain point of view, IBM is worse . . . flooding the world with ever more advanced computers, while its employees have no influence over what their product does to the human soul and to human society." Havel, like Orwell before him, typifies the anticommunist hero whose socialistic sentiments we love to forget. He also typifies an intelligence that looks beyond the bugbear of technology to the larger issues of its production, purpose, and distribution.

I think of those issues at the public library, where I sometimes go to do online research because the Internet service at my house is so erratic and slow. There I have the privilege of sitting with some of "the losers" who either do not have their own computers or lack Internet access at home (roughly a quarter of the U.S. adult population in both cases, with disproportionate representation by minorities, the poor, the aged, and the disabled). The first thought that occurs to me is the fallacy of promoting technology as an equalizer in a society of systemic inequality. Them that's got shall upgrade, and them that's not shall fall further behind.

But paradoxically the losers might actually enjoy more online privacy than some of their "betters" do. This is because they engage technology in the sphere of public rather than private property. Google knows less about them than it does about their dentist—and is certainly not bothered by that fact because losers generate less revenue than dentists. But losers also raise an important question, one already raised in this book, which is whether privacy and private are such natural bedfellows as we like to think.

As for the uneasy fellowship of privacy and technology, it cannot be parsed without addressing larger economic and spiritual issues. "The fault, dear Brutus, is not in the stars but in ourselves," and the ding, dear reader, is not in the universe but in our heads. It was there long before anyone thought of implanting an Internet chip in the same spot, though it contributed mightily to the suggestion.

16

STORIES THAT BEGIN IN AIRPORTS
PRIVACY, SUSTAINABILITY, AND RESISTANCE

> None of us know all the potentialities that slumber in the
> spirit of the population, or all the ways in which that popu-
> lation can surprise us when there is the right interplay of
> events.
>
> —VÁCLAV HAVEL, *DISTURBING THE PEACE*

What is indisputably new, if we insist on novelty, is the human ability to destroy life on Earth. As a result of that fact,
nearly every political, economic, and technological issue we
face is of necessity an environmental issue as well. That is
certainly true of privacy.

Many of the ways in which we maintain our privacy are
simply not sustainable. Palatial houses that permit their
members solitary occupancy of multiple rooms (the size of a
typical American home doubled between 1950 and 2000,
from 983 to over 2,200 square feet), second and third homes
that allow for greater public invisibility, arable land waste-
fully used as a buffer between neighbors, private automobiles
as the norm for commuting to work, periodic escape to remote locales via carbon-based transportation, to say nothing
of the coal-and-nuclear–enabled wiring with which we spin
our digital cocoons of virtual community—none of these in-
dulgences are compatible with the objective of achieving a
just and sustainable world. That granted, it might seem as
though privacy will ultimately have to be sacrificed for the
environment, and perhaps to some degree it will. But it might
also be that people committed to preserving the environment

will need to pay more attention to issues of privacy if ever they hope to gain popular support.

A focus on the protection of privacy as an environmental imperative would include the recognition that subsistence cultures have a great deal to teach us about how to maintain privacy through nonmaterial means, about how individuals can live close to one another without living on one another's backs. Add to this the recognition that enabling people to cultivate rich private lives may have as much environmental efficacy as developing a better solar storage cell. I have written elsewhere that our environment is threatened less by people who say "not in my backyard" (NIMBY) to alternative energy projects than by people who are never in their backyards. Movement tends to generate carbon. But staying put can be an attractive proposition only for those who feel let alone in a chosen, cherished place.

Not least of all, an environmentalist agenda that took account of privacy would include the recognition that environmentalists and privacy rights advocates might sometimes be united in their renunciations. Many of those who have set up green households, for example, or attempted to form environmentally sustainable communities are also seeking to limit their engagement with the peekaboo economy and the surveillance state. "Those who choose to live off the grid," writes Nick Rosen in his recent study of that subculture, "tend to be private." And even those who tend otherwise might eventually come to appreciate the virtues of privacy, as witnessed by the history of countercultural communes in the United States and successive generations of kibbutzim in Israel-Palestine. Suspect and even discouraged at first, privacy usually made a comeback.

Sometimes I imagine a man and a woman meeting each other for the first time in an airport bar. Both of them are in need of a drink because both of them have just missed their flights. In fact, they have chosen to miss their flights, and since both live in the United States, where missing a flight has roughly the same implications as dying unshriven had for a medieval Catholic, both are feeling a bit giddy just to be alive.

"It was the carbon," the woman says after her first sip. "Well over a ton of the stuff from New York to London, and that's *per passenger*. I'd have to drive my car three times across the continental United States to match it. I simply couldn't justify that to myself anymore."

The man is impressed, though his reason is different. "It was the strip-search business that did it for me. If that's what it costs to fly, then flight can take a flying you-know-what."

I will spare you the account of how they fall in love and of the fierce daughter born to them and the revolution she grows up to lead. Instead, I will make a statement that will seem to contradict a repeated contention of this book. Notwithstanding my protests to the contrary, there is at least one way in which I'm willing to grant that privacy is an elitist issue. The same charge is sometimes leveled against environmentalism, and the charge sticks there as well, and for the same reason. The elitism I have in mind is not based upon class or color, but upon character, the only criterion by which Martin Luther King was willing to have his children judged. Privacy and sustainability both belong by first right to the oldest elite the world has ever known, by which I mean the aristocracy of those who can do without. Writing on behalf of that aristocracy, Henry David Thoreau said we are wealthy in proportion to the number of things we "can afford to let alone." He might have been speaking of himself or of the !Kung or of the old farmer I knew who used to walk the steep mountain road down from his unwired house to the general store in the valley and count out the price of his Saturday-night quart of Schaefer's from an oval plastic change purse. You know one when you meet one, and on the same gut level as a lapdog knows a wolf. The old man would take a ride if offered, sometimes, but he never hitch-hiked, and he didn't share much in the way of personal information. He didn't need a ride that bad.

•

I do not think it is wrong to admire people like that. I think it is wrong and reactionary to speak of them as a vanishing breed. If the lapdog recognizes the wolf, it is because a wolf survives in him too. This is why mass movements of resistance and private acts of refusal are not mutually exclusive.

In December of 2010, air traveler John Tyner made national news by refusing a pat-down with the words "You touch my junk, and I'm going to have you arrested." Others joined Tyner in resisting intrusive body searches and in refusing to enter one of the 385 full-body scanners then installed in 68 of the largest U.S. airports to clear passengers for boarding. The choice offered was between a virtual strip search in one of these machines or a physical pat-down by an airport security officer. Tyner resisted both. Two months later, in response to public outcry, President Obama asked the Transportation Security Administration to review its screening procedures.

This involved retesting a previously rejected "blob" machine, so named because the image it revealed was less anatomically explicit than that of the "naked" machine adopted by the U.S. Department of Homeland Security with no input from the citizens footing the bill. Why the agency had made this choice, when both technologies were developed by the same firm and shown to be "equally effective at identifying contraband," remains open to speculation. I suspect two factors came into play. The first was the hope of discouraging Muslims from flying, or at the least of coercing them to accept pat-downs without risking the appearance of racial profiling. (The pat-downs were performed by persons of the passenger's gender, whereas the gender of the person monitoring a body scan was never specified.) I believe the second motivation was to determine just how malleable the American people had become in an "age of terror." By and large they had already accepted preemptive war in Iraq, prisoners held without trial at Guantánamo Bay, extraordinary rendition to the torture chambers of brutal regimes, and FBI scrutiny of their library cards. Might they accept a strip search too, provided it was justified in the name of national security and blessed by the sanctifying aura of the All-High-Tech? Apparently not.

There is hope in that. To venture once more into the realm of hypothesis, I would suggest that the passengers who resisted the naked machines were cut from the same cloth as the passengers who prevented United Airlines Flight 93 from ever making it to Washington. In other words, I would suggest that those who vilified John Tyner's refusal as an unacceptable self-indulgence given the "ever-looming threat of terror" were grossly missing the point. We do not enhance national security by fostering a culture of passivity and compliance.

On a less dramatic scale, the periodic blowbacks by Facebook users outraged over such changes as the opening of the site to the general public in 2006, the Beacon feature of 2007 (which automatically posted users' activities on other sites to Facebook), and the 2009 changes to the site's terms of use (a subversion of users' ownership of their information) demonstrate that the will to resist may still be there. Admittedly, these protests seem only a little less pathetic than those of junkies pleading with their pusher to provide them with a better class of junk. Knowing their need for his product, he also knows that given enough time they will come around to his point of view. This certainly seems to have been Mark Zuckerberg's assumption, as evidenced through a well-documented pattern of public apologies, policy overhauls, and further breaches of privacy.

One can imagine more muscular forms of revolt. Much has been made of the use of digital communication in coordinating resistance to oppressive governments in Egypt and Libya. I wonder how effectively digital communication might be used against itself—by which I mean against those who trample privacy rights for profit. Saturating social media with misinformation (sifted and decoded for one's real friends by low-tech means), matching every pertinent web search with at least three bogus searches, and blog-posting these intentions along with petitions to boycott all products pitched through data mining might show the windows of the digital Panopticon to be as vulnerable as the bricks in the Berlin Wall. Corporate sponsors would remain largely untouched, of course, but stronger acts of resistance might follow the edifying sight of their scurrying out of the cybersphere like rats from a sinking ship.

To those who would judge such forms of resistance unlikely, I can say only that prior to their appearance, I'd have said the Arab Spring and the Occupy Wall Street movement were unlikely too. And we should remember that at least some of the resistance undertaken in defense of privacy is also private and therefore unknown to most of us. We do at least know the common denominator in all acts of resistance. All of them are marked by a willingness to bear some inconvenience. All of them involve a conscious choice to do without.

Not surprisingly, this also turns out to be the common denominator in what we might call a sense of the sacred. Think of anything to which the word *sacredness* might apply, and immediately you conjure up instances of freely chosen inconvenience. Pilgrimages, moments of silence, courtships, wedding ceremonies, bar mitzvahs, graduations, hunger strikes, car pools, recycling stations, twenty-one-gun salutes, cemeteries (ever watch somebody mow around those stones?)—all are bothersome, highly impractical, extremely unbusinesslike acts of inconvenience that people nevertheless undertake in order to express their conviction that certain values take precedence over their immediate needs and desires.

When people complain that nothing is sacred anymore, they are essentially saying that we are at the point where nothing trumps convenience. They are lamenting that what has come to matter most is getting what we want in the best, cheapest, and quickest manner possible. In a roundabout way they are also talking about technology, consumer capitalism, the fate of the earth, and the will to resist. Almost always they are talking about privacy, about the explicit exposure of matters they feel ought to be kept private.

In essence they are raising what may be the central question about the right of privacy, which is not about how best to encrypt our e-mail messages or how best to legislate against online identity theft. The central question is whether we hold our privacy sacred enough to endure the inconveniences necessary to preserve it. Or perhaps the central question is whether such a thing as sacredness even exists in what Americans, with characteristic solipsism, refer to as "our post-9/11 world."

17

BODY AND SOUL

A FINAL CONTRARIAN ARGUMENT

> Yet it seems to me, on the darkest nights, and sometimes
> in the clear light of day, that we are losing the ethos that
> has sustained what is most to be valued in our civilization.
> —MARILYNNE ROBINSON,
> "NIGHT THOUGHTS OF A BAFFLED HUMANIST"

Aside from launching a preemptive war, the two most notable U.S. responses to the terrorist attacks of 9/11 were a weakening of privacy rights and the use of torture. People marveled—Osama bin Laden himself is supposed to have marveled—at the ease with which the Twin Towers collapsed on themselves, but future generations may marvel even more at the quick collapses signified by the passage of the USA Patriot Act and the photos out of Abu Ghraib.

The developments were related, and related by more than being drastic measures for drastic threats. They shared a common philosophical foundation—or we might rather say, they lacked a common philosophical foundation, by which I mean the humanism that informs the nation's founding documents. Mediated through the Enlightenment, and with roots in older religious and philosophical traditions, this humanism is expressed most memorably in the preamble to the Declaration of Independence and more flamboyantly in Hegel: "Even the criminal thought of a malefactor has more grandeur and nobility than the wonders of heaven." The quotation happens to have been a favorite of Karl Marx. Thomas Paine would have had no trouble drinking to it.

But "grandeur and nobility" have been on the ropes for some time. Postmodern theorists were jabbing at them when Osama bin Laden was still a client of the CIA. While it is unfair to blame a handful of academics for creating a nihilism they had merely, if gleefully, appropriated from the broader culture—like blaming Darwin because one doesn't like the look of Galápagos tortoises—it is even more unfair to claim that postmodernism became irrelevant after 9/11. With smoke still rising from the ruins of the World Trade Center, conservative pundits were quick to claim just that. Apparently still rattled by the explosions, the pundits could not have been more wrong.

In fact, the postmodern era was being born even as they were writing its obituary. The academics they despised had made the annunciation, and their patrons in Washington were assisting at the birth. No more "master narratives" beginning with the once-upon-a-time of "We hold these truths to be self-evident." No more "absolutist" prohibitions on the field of war. No more Eurocentric Latinisms like habeas corpus. The barbarians were at the gate, and lest we be found wanting in multicultural protocol, we would go out to meet them in the guise of barbarians.

The relaxation of "acceptable limits" that allowed for illegal surveillance at home and waterboarding abroad were related in function as well as in philosophy. The dismantling of humanism is in practice the dismantling of a human being. One can define the inhumanity of torture as the most extreme invasion of privacy, an attempt to own the victim's body even to its tiniest nerve ending, an attempt to know her soul. As Elaine Scarry notes in *The Body in Pain,* torture forces the prisoner "to attend to the most intimate and interior facts of his body (pain, hunger, nausea, sexuality, excretion) at a time when there is no benign privacy, for he is under constant surveillance, and there is no benign public . . . only an ugly inverting of the two." A part of this inverting is the desecration of the domestic sphere, the sphere of private life, often achieved by the use of common household objects—doorknobs, chairs, bathtubs—as props in the torment.

The illegal intercepts performed with the cooperation of Verizon and AT&T and the extraordinary renditions performed with the cooperation of Egypt and Jordan were thus on a continuum. The justification was utilitarian—as was opposition to torture on the moral low ground of "it doesn't work"—but the sales pitch was pure technocratic consumerism, convenience at any price: the information we need, when we need it, as soon as we need it, and by any means available. Like snail mail, humanism was a quaint and cumbersome indulgence we could no longer afford. We were obliged to get beyond the old rights-based pieties; we needed to think outside the box, if only to accept the necessity of putting a living man into one. Arms raised passively in an airport security scan, we too entered the box. The so-called dignity of the human person was as obsolete as a typewriter. "Privacy," declared an op-ed in *The Washington Post*, "is so 1997"—not that far removed from saying, as our political leaders seemed to be saying, that the notion of a war crime is so 1946. Why stop there? The Emancipation Proclamation—so 1863.

The common theme that runs through the War on Terror and the postmodern age that spawned it is the testing of boundaries, a "Why on earth not?" approach to any stricture seen as limiting the fullest exercise of whim. The mortal limits of what a human being can bear, the constitutional limits of what a government may do, the social limits of what one human being is entitled to know about another—in short, any ethical restraints upon the will to power—are meant to be pushed.

In such a context, private blurs with public; interrogation techniques blur with performance art. Wondering where it might take me, I read Lauren Berlant and Michael Warner's essay "Sex in Public," spurred on by the first arresting subhead: "There Is Nothing More Public Than Privacy." By "sex" they do not mean sex acts per se but the "heteronormative" assumptions that dominate public life. So far, so good—except that domination also turns out to have blurry boundaries. By the essay's climax, for which there can be no better word, the professors are attending a leather bar performance of "ferocity and abjection . . . trust and violation" that leaves them utterly transfixed. For the delectation of a crowd "moaning softly with admiration, then whistling, stomping, screaming encouragements," a dominant male methodically pours various foods and fluids down the throat of a "twentyish, very skateboard" boy sitting in a restraining chair until, with the help of three fingers inserted into his dog-collared throat, the slave begins vomiting on the proffered stomach of his master. The marvel of it all is that the boy is the only one in the joint who vomits.

"We are breathless," the authors write. "But, good academics that we are, we also have some questions to ask. Word has gone around that the boy is straight. We want to know: What does this mean in this context? How did you discover that this is what you want to do? How did you find a male top to do it with?" Since when does one need to be a "good academic" to ask these kinds of questions? A middling short-order cook might have managed to find both the questions and the exit a whole lot quicker. No matter, the possibility that the "twentyish" boy might be exploited has as much effect on the discourse as would a rumor that the bartender was wearing a toupee. Professor Laura Kipnis is a good deal less coy when she comments in *The New York Times* on a "boundary-crossing" photo-performance she'd staged as an art student. "I cast a homeless man as the romantic heroine and had him wear a frilly dress and say romantic clichés. I did pay him, of course."

I'm sure there were nuances to both of these performances that are lost on me. I'm sure there were similar nuances in public exhibitions of the Elephant Man and the Hottentot Venus. I'm sure I don't care. Those who see privacy as the realm of abuse need to look again. Abuse has always been as public as private: hiding in the disingenuous innocence of "nothing to hide," the façade of "consent" with an economic gun to its back. But I'm driving at something else.

The main question these performances raise for me is this: At what point does the Fourth Amendment's protection against "unreasonable searches and seizures" and the judicial phrase "offensive to a reasonable person," a common rule of thumb in privacy cases, lose all meaning? Or to put it more directly, at what point does the reasonable person herself lose all value? At what point does "the steady hemorrhage of meaning and value from human existence" with which Terry Eagleton characterizes late-capitalist societies spend its last drop of blood? Were the photos that came out of Abu Ghraib "offensive to a reasonable person"? Would it help to call them art? Would it help to know that the hooded figure of the reasonable person standing on the box had been paid? How much? I mean how much would it help?

•

We speak of privacy as a right, but we might also think of it as a test, as a canary in the mine of our civilization. It lives or dies to the extent that we remain willing to believe that the human person, body and soul—our blood relative in his or her flesh, and beyond reduction in his or her grandeur and nobility—is sacred, endowed with inalienable rights, and a microcosm of us all. Privacy lives or dies to the extent that we can without vomiting use a phrase like "the sanctity of a human being."

On many levels we still do. Even our most bitter political arguments, including those related to privacy, are not without humanistic preconceptions. The abortion debate is a case in point. Both sides rely on a sense of human sacredness, though they locate its center in different places. The right to life and the right of bodily self-determination are not oppositional in their basic foundations. Reproductive freedom rests on a right of privacy, which rests in turn on the notional sanctity of a human life. The Supreme Court used the word *spiritual* in *Planned Parenthood v. Casey* (1992), which *extended* the protections of *Roe v. Wade* (1973), declaring that "The destiny of the woman must be shaped to a large extent on her own conception of her spiritual imperatives and her place in society." The pro-life position and the pro-choice position are as locked in mutually assured destruction as any two superpowers with nuclear arms, though I would prefer to think of arms here in the sense of a wrestling embrace. Neither side can blow the doctrinal ground out from under the other without doing the same to its own.

But the possibility of engineering a child into a "posthuman" creature, of hardwiring the decisional privacy of the mother into the World Wide Web, moves the debate onto radically different ground. It is the ground envisioned by the likes of MIT professor Bruce Mazlish, a world "inhabited solely by humans and machines" in which man "eradicates the animal in himself," and probably animals in general, while transcending "the 'base' necessity of bowel movements, or perhaps even of sex." At that point the final boundary to be tested is the boundary of humanness itself.

The ultimate debate over privacy is not between Roe and Wade; it is between Jane Austen and zombies. It is between Erasmus and the Terminator. The privacy-defining struggle of the future will not be waged between liberty-loving Americans and dignity-loving Europeans, or between champions of the Fourth Amendment and champions of the First. It will be waged between a ragtag coalition of humanists and those who will not accept humanism without a prefix—be it *post*, *trans*, *anti*, or *in*—much less any boundary between human and machine, between evolution and invention, between a person's most intimate secrets and what "everybody has a right to know."

Needless to say, the conflict will be driven by market forces. Adam Smith's "invisible hand," which we believe in more than Moses believed in the hand of God, will deal the cards. Just as competition is a precondition of survival in the marketplace, engineered enhancements of the human person will become a precondition of competitive viability. No Internet chip in your head? You're really gonna need one of those if you want to get into a good college. Broad-based resistance to global capitalism, if it comes, will not arise because global capitalism creates poverty, destroys indigenous cultures, and degrades the environment, though global capitalism will continue to do all three. Resistance will come, if it comes, because global capitalism in its final form will force upon us the choice between retaining our creaturely integrity or literally *incorporating* the innovations of the market into our nerve endings and bones.

Global capitalism will be overthrown, if it is overthrown,

not in the hopes of establishing utopia, but as the result of a collective resistance to utopia—to the faux heaven of unbounded self-indulgence and the biotechnological nightmare of everlasting life. People will die fighting for the right to die. People will die fighting to preserve death and birth in some semblance of the intimacy befitting human relationships and the privacy befitting a human being.

Or they will go with the flow. They will be paid, of course.

•

Around the same time as I began reading books addressing the heady question "What is privacy?" my adult daughter, then employed as a counselor at a socially progressive summer camp, upped the conceptual ante by introducing me to the question "What is a woman?" (She also introduced me to the term "hetero-normative," which would prove of some help in reading an article mentioned above.) The question and the term had both been raised during a fireside discussion among her fellow counselors, along with the sometimes vexing matter of which personal pronouns each of them preferred to go by.

As befitting a father with an intelligent adult daughter, I kept my mouth shut and listened. But I found myself wanting to say, "Do you want to know what a woman is? I can tell you what a woman is. A woman is a person who still earns seventy-seven cents an hour for every dollar that a man earns. A woman is a person who, if she lives in the United States, has a one-in-four chance of being sexually assaulted some time in her life. A woman is a person who, if she lives in Afghanistan, has an even better chance of being splashed with acid if she so much as shows her face. And do you want to know something else? The men who pay the woman the seventy-seven cents, and rape her on car hoods, and splash acid on her face—not a one of them, rest assured, has the slightest trouble whatsoever figuring out what a woman is. They got that one down. They *never* get it wrong. What's a woman, was that the question? A woman is the most pathetic creature on the face of God's earth if the best she can say for herself after ten thousand years of struggle is 'What's a woman?' "

But I kept quiet, as I said, if only because I could tell from the tone of bemused skepticism I have learned to recognize and come to love in my daughter's voice that she didn't need me to say a word. In fact, it would not surprise me to learn that during the discussion at camp she had said something similar to what her old man was thinking—and challenged it in the same breath—though some of what her old man was thinking had to do with images dating from before her time. I was thinking of black men in jackets and ties carrying signs through Memphis, Tennessee, that read I AM A MAN. Many of my color were prepared to resist the implications of that statement, but no one could pretend not to understand what it meant. "Ain't I a woman?" asked Sojourner Truth, in a tone that implied "What the hell else would I be?" On the day when people begin asking "What's a human being?" it will be time for me to die. I would add "preferably with some privacy," except that, if human nature itself is in doubt, privacy will be long gone.

18

ANOTHER NATIVITY

A CONCLUSION

I would not open any doore upon you, but look in when
you open it.

— JOHN DONNE, IN A LETTER

Were I a Zen master wanting to teach a Zen of privacy, I
would set my pupils the task of meditating on this koan: "A
pregnant woman gets onto a bus."

If any image is capable of scrambling our notions of private and public in a hurry, of obliterating our nicest definitions in one satori-like flash, it is the sight of a woman great
with child. Her condition is an unequivocally public statement of a very private experience, begun in circumstances of
intimacy and continued within the sanctum of her own
body—yet there is no hiding it for her, nor any denying the
feeling we have that somehow she belongs to us, that she
embodies our collective future and represents our individual
pasts. We depend on her even more than on the mail carrier
to get us our Social Security checks on time, and she depends
on us for the social security of her child, albeit with an increasingly dubious reliability. And she is—she has to be—
poignantly aware of all this.

She moves down the aisle like a ticking bomb. Elbows are
pulled in, perhaps a seat is offered. At any moment she could
give birth in the midst of us, lacking so much as a !Kung
woman's prerogative to take her labor pains into the privacy
of the bush. None of us, not even a mother of ten, knows exactly what she is feeling, or what or if the life within her
feels, or what she thinks from moment to moment. She is

completely out there and almost as completely hidden from view—like all of us, really. Montaigne says that there is "nothing more unsociable than Man, and nothing more sociable." And she is acutely aware of that too.

I interviewed two pregnant women in the course of writing this book. The younger of them, pregnant for the first time, expressed her amazement at the kinds of questions she was asked by strangers—but only when she was alone. Was the pregnancy planned? Was she going to breastfeed? Had she picked out names? Had she and her husband been particularly bored during the long winter nights? As the elder of the two women, pregnant for her second time, would observe: "People like to talk about deep personal things." And sometimes show a want of depth when they do.

I spoke to the second woman in New York, in a restaurant where we waited for three other people to join us for dinner. We had arrived early in order to conduct our conversation in private.

She was close to her delivery date when we met. She and her husband had already made a number of decisions relating to the birth. It would take place in a hospital with a midwife in attendance. If and when the time came to hold her hand, her husband would be there to do it. A circle of Iranian exiles on whose behalf the couple is active would not be present, though they had offered to come, as they would have done in Iran, the women gathering in the room and the men waiting to celebrate out in the hall. As she explained to them, this was not generally the custom in the United States. We have different notions of privacy, though that is not to say that the Iranians have no notion at all. I would not be welcome to attend the birth of my choice in Iran.

The woman and her husband had also decided, or rather she had decided and he had readily concurred, that she would not discuss the possible effects upon her fetus of the toxoplasmosis she had contracted during the pregnancy, not until testing revealed whether the toxins had passed to the fetus. The condition would not harm the mother, or any of us if we contracted it; it could only do harm to a fetus if contracted during pregnancy. But what that harm might be she would not discuss with friends or with physicians either. Nor would she and her husband discuss the option of termination, even with each other, until the test results were known. That was their pact.

"People don't like you not to know things," she told me. "I wanted the privacy of not knowing. And your doctors and your friends don't want you to not know anything. They want you to know everything." *Everything* turned out to be blindness and severe brain damage—but not for this baby, who, as tests revealed after five weeks of agonized waiting, was not affected. Needless to say, the woman remained affected by the experience, and on multiple levels. "The idea that you don't want to talk about something incredibly terrifying and personal and real is so un-American."

She came by the word naturally. A self-described "second-generation Red-diaper baby," though without any illusions about what she had seen firsthand during years of working as an American journalist in Eastern Europe, she grew up hearing the story of how her physicist grandfather had been jailed for refusing to name names during the McCarthy era. Knowing a subpoena would eventually come for her as well, and that a consequence of imprisonment would be losing her children to foster care, the grandmother had taken them into hiding until the trouble passed. My companion attributes her father's lifelong reticence to that boyhood exodus. He is known for never supplying more information than is necessary.

The grandfather was eventually released, though his career was ruined. Years afterward, one of his grandsons was questioned by a classmate after hearing a familiar surname during a classroom roll call. Assured as to the grandson's identity, the classmate said, "Your grandpa went to jail so mine wouldn't have to." In other words, your grandfather had refused to make a private matter public.

I'd have liked to talk to the grandfather as well, but he has long since passed on. I'd have liked to ask him what privacy he had known in the privation that was prison. I suspect he would not have known much, but I also suspect he would have been able to recall at least a few instances, all the more precious for having been so rare, of privacy honored intentionally and to the minimal degree that circumstances allowed. Over the years I have become an amateur collector of those fragile flowers.

English explorers in the sixteenth century capture an Inuit man and shortly thereafter a woman and her infant. "Now that we had a native woman for the comfort of the man we had captured earlier, we brought them both together, with our men watching silently to observe the nature of their meeting." The prisoners behave with humdrum dignity, caring for each other throughout the imprisonment that will prove fatal to them both, yet "they never used each other as man and wife" and "all the while were so modest" and "most careful that their private parts were not exposed to each other or to anyone else."

Four gunmen go on a rampage and force patrons at a diner to strip naked and perform sex acts on the floor. Those who refuse are beaten. Knowledge is not power here, and there is pitiably little knowledge, as little knowledge as pity, and only the flimsiest of choices left to the victims in their powerlessness. They all decide the same way. As one survivor recalls, contrasting the experience with that of being on a nude beach, "Nobody looked."

Two lovers have a spat on a crowded city street. Passersby give them room, look away; this is not their quarrel. Do the lovers feel lonelier to have that discretion added to their rift? Or does it reconnect them to their community, assuring them that there are decent people out there, sidewalks full of them in fact, no matter if the trouble between them passes or hardens into something worse?

Social workers intervene in a case of extreme hoarding, entering rooms that have grown so packed, squalid, and infested that body suits and respirator gear are required. For the tearful occupant this is an apocalypse, the end of the world. Yet those playing the angels try their best to behave like guests. They lay hands on what a reasonable person would recognize as a keepsake. They lay it aside for safekeeping.

Japanese Americans, interned during the Second World War, "didn't even have separate toilets. We had a long row of holes and it was very difficult. . . . Most of us waited until the wee hours to go to the bathroom to do bowel movements, because we didn't want to be sitting there to the whole world." And yet if two met at the latrines in the wee hours, it was surely not to gawk. The act of averting one's eyes from a neighbor's forced exposure and the act of refusing to turn away from a neighbor's need—are they not at bottom the same act?

When the Nazis overran the British Channel Islands, they deported some of the residents to internment camps in southern Germany. "Some people were able to adjust to their circumstances, but the incessant noise . . . overcrowded rooms and lack of privacy were more problematic for others. One of the most popular types of artifacts to be made from the raw materials of the Red Cross parcel was the trinket box. As a private possession for storing personal items, this seemed to form a kind of material antidote to communal life lived perpetually under the gaze of other people."

I keep these stories in a mental trinket box. Some of them I share; others must remain hidden away.

After I have put the period on my last sentence, I will phone the woman I interviewed in the restaurant and congratulate her on the birth of a healthy son, born last week as I write. I will not ask what was decided in regard to circumcision, though I know that she, Jewish by background, was leaving that decision to her husband, Catholic by background, "because he has a penis and I don't." Nor will I ask with what words she managed to fend off the offers of well-meaning friends, to host a bris in one instance, to share a tasty recipe for placenta in another. I'm confident that, as with the Iranians, she's managed just fine.

Instead I will ask if she will read what I have written about her, as per our prior arrangement. If her permission extends that far, you may even know her name. Possibly you will not read this at all. I will have written it in the most extreme zone of privacy a writer can know. In such a case, I will need to start over from scratch and proceed in a different way, but I will do my best to arrive at the same conclusion.

In this book I have tried to flesh out the meaning of privacy. I have located its basis in the bodily integrity of human beings and in their spiritual needs. I have defined it in terms of resistance to exploitation. I have argued, as have many before me, that it is essential to a democracy. I have suggested that it might be placed on an even stronger footing in a more social democracy. At the end of the day, however, privacy may amount to little more, and rest on no firmer basis, than the promises we make to one another. Privacy being what it is, they are kept more often than we know.

NOTES

1. LET'S BEGIN BY DOING A LITTLE SHARING

1   *"Man did not enter"* Paine, *Common Sense,* 89.

3   *"Perhaps the most striking"* Thomson, "The Right to Privacy," 1.

3   *"Let me alone"* Supreme Court Justice Louis D. Brandeis famously called "the right to be let alone" the "most comprehensive of rights and the right most valued by civilized men" (*Olmstead v. United States,* 1928).

2. FRIENDS AND ENEMIES

4   *Emerson* Westin, *Privacy and Freedom,* 38.

5   *Tyler Clementi* Aboujaoude, "Violin Requiem for Privacy"; Kirn, "Little Brother Is Watching." The male student who used his webcam to spy on Clementi was found guilty of privacy violation and anti-gay intimidation in March 2012.

6   *our transgressions* In *Dreaming Up America* Russell Banks identifies the Fountain of Youth as perhaps the strongest of three American dreams (the others being El Dorado and the City on the Hill) because "it carries within it the sense of the new, the dream of starting over, of having a New Life" (7).

6   *Yahoo* Rebecca MacKinnon, "Shi Tao, Yahoo!"

6   *Google* "Beginning in 2004, [Google] arranged to tweak and twist its algorithms and filter its results so that the native-language Google.cn would omit results unwelcome to the [Chinese] government." Gleick, "How Google Dominates Us," 26.

6   *Verizon* Helft and Miller, "1986 Privacy Law Is Outrun by the Web."

6   *USA Patriot Act* Frederick S. Lane, *American Privacy,* 248.

6   *4 percent of all U.S. libraries* Scarry, *Rule of Law,* 29.

6   *National Security Agency* Priest and Arkin, "A Hidden World, Growing Beyond Control."

7   *Google's . . . revenue* Gleick, 25.
7   *"Open Planet"* Jeffrey Rosen, *The Deciders*, 1–4.
7   *"Little Brother"* Kirn.
7   *keylogger* Aboujaoude.
8   *a tyrant does not need* Tocqueville, *Democracy in America*, 109.
8   *Lower Merion, Pennsylvania* Martin, "Lower Merion District's Laptop Saga," *Robbins v. Lower Merion School District* (2010).
8   *Chairman Mao* "Mao Thinks Well of Nixon."
9   *Clementi had already come out* Ian Parker, "The Story of a Suicide," 44.
11   *hippie communes* Timothy Miller, *The 60s Communes*, 194–95.
11   *Loud family* See Hefferman, "Too Much Vérité," on the Louds in retrospect. "We haven't learned a thing. We're still distorting relationships to document them. . . . Digital cameras have turned every family into the Louds."

3. PENUMBRAS

14   *"I love living"* Montaigne, "On Vanity," 1117–18.
14   *common linguistic root* Williams, *Keywords*, 242.
15   *English word* McDougall, 139. Its first recorded appearance is in 1450. According to the author it has over 100 definitions.
15   *no language does* Webb, *Privacy and Solitude in the Middle Ages*, xvi.
16   *"A Bachelor's Complaint"* Lamb, *Essays of Elia*, 154–61.
16   *Bedouin women* Abu-Lughod, *Veiled Sentiments*, 159–67.
17   *"Is privacy a situation"* Karst, "Right of Privacy," 2242.
17   *"like many legal concepts"* Gerety, "Right of Privacy (update)," 2248.
17   *front yards* The distinction is noted in van Manen and Levering, *Childhood's Secrets*, 60.
17   *"No human life"* Arendt, *The Human Condition*, 22.
18   *"interdependent chambers"* Smith, *Private Matters*, 237. Lloyd Weinreb says that the public-private distinction is "scarcely more than [a] reminder that human beings are at one and the same time constituted as persons within a human community and autonomous." Cited in Greene, "Beyond *Lawrence*," 1898.

18   *privacy with secrecy* van Manen and Levering, 73.

18   *"hidden information"* Kelly, *The Psychology of Secrets*, 4–5.

18   *Sociologists* McDougall, 188, citing a study by Carol Warren and Barbara Lalett.

18   *the age of four* Saltz, *Anatomy of a Secret Life*, 12.

18   *resistance to governmental intrusion* "Where a compelling interest is shown, privacy provides a regulatory standard against which the maximum intrusion permitted the state is the minimum necessary to satisfy its interest." Samar, *The Right to Privacy*, 142.

19   *school principal* I'm alluding to *Safford Unified School District v. Redding* (2009), in which the Supreme Court ruled in favor of a high school student whose principal had ordered her strip-searched because another student had claimed she was carrying drugs. Cited in Jeffrey Rosen, *The Deciders*, 6.

19   *"Privacy protects love"* Inness, *Privacy, Intimacy, and Isolation*, 12.

19   *Alan Westin identifies* Westin, *Privacy and Freedom*, 31.

19   *Anita Allen speaks* Allen, *Uneasy Access*, 60.

19   *DeCew* Young, *On Female Body Experience*, 164.

19   *Whalen v. Roe* Quoted in Karst, "Right of Privacy," 2242.

20   *Prosser's list* Nimmer, "Privacy and the First Amendment," 2014.

20   *Solove's approach* Solove, *Understanding Privacy*, 8–9, 42–44.

21   *somehow antisocial* Solove, *Understanding Privacy*, 5. "Legal Scholar Fred Cate declares that privacy is 'an antisocial construct . . . [that] conflicts with other important values within the society.'"

21   *"much theoretical discussion"* Young, 164.

22   *Reiman* Greene, 1898.

22   *"our very integrity as persons"* Fried, "Privacy," 477.

22   *Douglas's words* Karst, "Right of Privacy," 2242.

4. GETTING YOUR DEGREE

24   *"What a heavy burden"* "Celebrity," 15.

24   *Oliver Sipple* Whitman, "The Two Western Cultures of Privacy," 1196. Sipple eventually committed suicide.

24   *a 1985 French case* Whitman, 1197.

25   *"no legitimate expectations"* Jeffrey Rosen, *Deciders*, 2.

25   *Justice Harlan* Solove, "A Brief History of Information Privacy Law," 1-22.

25   *"The home is the one place"* Allen and Mack, "How Privacy Got Its Gender," 467.

26   *Lillian Jones* Friedman, *Guarding Life's Dark Secrets*, 224.

26   *In 1982 a woman* Alderman and Kennedy, *The Right to Privacy*, 171.

27   *Hottentot Venus* Koestenbaum, *Humiliation*, 135.

27   *Veronia School District* Whitman, 1202.

27   *1986 Louisiana court case* Alderman and Kennedy, 267.

28   *a liberty-based concept* Whitman, 1160–64.

29   *Zacchini v. Scripps-Howard Broadcasting Co.* Nimmer, "Privacy and the First Amendment," 2014.

30   *Lewis v. Dayton* Allen and Mack, 478.

31   *"You know your own degrees"* Macbeth III, iv.

31   *Madonna* "Celebrity," 85.

32   *Flora Bell Graham* Friedman, 220.

5. PRUDERY 2.0

33   *"the place where we are right"* Amichai, "The Place Where We Are Right," 34.

33   *"the ecstasy of sanctimony"* Roth, *The Human Stain*, 2.

34   *adaptation of . . . Medea* Jeffers, *Cawdor and Medea*, 121.

34   *"the democracy of everyday life"* Shklar, *Ordinary Vices*, 77.

34   *Benjamin Franklin* Shklar, 72.

35   *"the unending game"* Shklar, 67.

35   *"any attempt to hide"* Shklar, 47

35   *"we ought to give up"* Shklar, 247–48.

35   *"the Constitutional requirement"* Scarry, *Rule of Law*, 9–10; 14.

35   *Donald Kerr* Associated Press, "U.S. Official: Privacy Must Be Redefined."

36   *patients who self-censor* Kelly, *The Psychology of Secrets*, 141–49.

36   *"themes as opposed to details"* Kelly, 205.

36   *coming-out phase* See Nan Alamilla Boyd, *Wide Open Town*, 164–65.

36   *Michel Foucault* James Miller, *The Passion of Michel Foucault,* 255.

36   *"system of double binds"* Sedgwick, *Epistemology of the Closet,* 69–70.

37   *"capacity for self-disclosure"* Auden, "The Joker in the Pack," *The Dyer's Hand and Other Essays,* 109–10.

39   *pathetic and humiliating* I mean for both parties. "The person doing the humiliation . . . is humiliated by the act." Koestenbaum, *Humiliation,* 9.

6. STANDING UP FOR PRIVACY

41   *"To realize the relative validity"* Schumpeter, *Capitalism, Socialism and Democracy,* 243.

42   *the Chinese word* McDougall, *Love-Letters and Privacy in Modern China,* 139.

43   *Christian Heller* Gifford, "Interview with Christain Heller."

43   *a refuge from the world* Lasch, *Women and the Common Life,* 94–95.

43   *"human kind / Cannot bear"* "Burnt Norton."

43   *"Hell is other people"* Rafay, "On the Margins of Freedom."

43   *misanthropy* Shklar, *Ordinary Vices,* 3.

44   *the seeds of genius* Storr, *Solitude,* especially chapter 8, "Separation, Isolation, and the Growth of the Imagination," 106–22.

44   *"a collective individuality"* Karst, "The Freedom of Intimate Association," 629.

44   *a need to withdraw* van Manen and Levering, *Childhood's Secrets,* 75–76.

45   *"Let him who cannot"* Bonhoeffer, *Life Together,* 57.

45   *John Adams* McCullough, *John Adams,* 207.

45   *"they did not want"* Kriseová, *Václav Havel,* 269.

46   *Jeremy Bentham* James Miller, *The Passion of Michel Foucault,* 220.

46   *a recent experiment* Singer, "Visible Man," 36.

46   *"Unmonitored release affirms"* Fried, "Privacy," 492–93.

47   *learned helplessness* Altman, "Privacy Regulation," 68.

47   *Le Chambon* Hallie, *Lest Innocent Blood Be Shed*, 197–98.
     See also Pierre Sauvage's 1989 documentary, *Weapons of the
     Spirit*.

48   *unchecked individualism* Tocqueville, *Democracy in Amer-
     ica*, 104.

48   *"American honor"* Tocqueville, 242–55.

49   *Nazis* Whitman, "The Two Western Cultures of Privacy,"
     1187–89.

50   *Duchess of Berry* Whitman, 1174.

7. IS PRIVACY A UNIVERSAL VALUE?

51   *"aesthetic and moral relativism"* Judt, *Ill Fares the Land*, 89.

52   *Gebusi* Donald Black, *Moral Time*, 143. See also Singer,
     "Visible Man," 33.

52   *"There is no privacy"* Fielder and King, *Sexual Paradox*, 109.

52   *"privacy is not something"* Shostak, *Nisa*, 8.

52   *Their own name* Thomas, *The Harmless People*, 24.

52   *eat and sleep together* Shostak, 8.

52   *"every person's footprints"* Fielder and King, 109.

52   *extramarital affairs* Shostak, 237–57.

52   *"it is hard to imagine"* Moore, *Privacy*, 73–74.

53   *"the right to be let alone"* Olmstead v. United States (1928).

53   *pregnant !Kung* Thomas, 159–60. See also Shostak, 161.

53   *rudeness* Thomas, 43.

53   *a !Kung "hug"* Thomas, 70, 166.

53   *"inhibited" about urinating* Thomas, 107–108.

53   *fireside gathering* Thomas, 185.

54   *dance and trance* Shostak, 9.

54   *Irwin Altman* Altman, "Privacy Regulation." "I hypothesize
     that all cultures have evolved mechanisms by which mem-
     bers can regulate privacy, but that the particular pattern of
     mechanisms may differ across cultures" (70).

54   *"selective control of access"* The examples are all from Alt-
     man, 72–78. Kenneth Karst also notes "rules of restraint and
     social distance" and the use of secret names among Austra-
     lian Aborigines. "Right of Privacy," 2245. For a recent study
     of Americans attempting to exercise the same "selective con-
     trol," see Christina Nippert-Eng's *Islands of Privacy*.

54 *Even animals* Westin, *Privacy and Freedom*, 8–11.

55 *Chicago police department* Alderman and Kennedy, *The Right to Privacy*, 3–18.

56 *strip-searching has continued* Johnson, "Crying *Wolfish*," 42–52.

8. THE PRIVACY OF THE GODS

59 *Goddes pryvetee* "The Miller's Tale," 3454.

59 *Acteon* Bulfinch, *The Age of Fable*, 37.

59 *Bathsheba* 2 Samuel 11–12.

59 *Krishna* Ghosh, *The Dance of Shiva and Other Tales from India*, 102–104.

59 *"No man shall see me, and live"* Exodus 33:20 (KJV).

59 *descendants of Cain* Genesis 11:1–9.

60 *men of Sodom* Genesis 19:1–11.

60 *Shiva* Ghosh, 107.

60 *Semele* Bulfinch, 160.

60 *Yahweh and Moses* Exodus 33:17–23 (KJV).

61 *"our Lord's privy counsel"* Julian of Norwich, *Revelation of Divine Love*, 82.

61 *"so familiar and courteous"* Julian of Norwich, 11.

61 *"And your Father"* Matthew 6:1–18 (NRSV). Compare to Hannah Arendt, who writes that "love, in distinction from friendship, is killed, or rather extinguished, the moment it is displayed in public" *The Human Condition* (51).

61 *Job* Job 7:19–20 (NRSV).

61 *Noah's son Ham* Genesis 9:20–27.

62 *Marx and Trotsky* Trotsky, *My Life*, 1, 538 (first and last pages of his autobiography). Marx used such phrases as "free spiritual production." Eagleton, *Why Marx Was Right*, 154.

9. NATIVITY

64 *"And she brought forth"* Luke 2:7 (KJV).

64 *1881* See discussion of *De May v. Roberts* below.

64 *Bill of Rights* Karst, "Right of Privacy," 2241.

65 *"I refute it thus"* Boswell, *Life of Samuel Johnson, L.L.D.*, 134.

65 *United States v. Jones* "Justices Say."

65   *"privacy case of the decade"* Rosen, "Interpreting the Constitution in the Digital Era."
66   *"most influential law review article"* Harry Kalven, Jr., quoted in Solove, "A Brief History of Information Privacy Law," 1–10.
66   *"add a chapter to our law"* Roscoe Pound quoted in Solove, "A Brief History of Information Privacy Law," 1–10.
66   *Some have suggested* Allen and Mack, "How Privacy Got Its Gender," 441–42; 455–57. The authors describe the article as "overwrought by today's standards." It is indeed.
66   *Athena* Allen and Mack, 441.
66   *the story goes* Whitman, "The Two Western Cultures of Privacy," 1204.
67   *"The press is overstepping"* Warren and Brandeis, "The Right to Privacy," 196.
67   *"sacred precincts"* Warren and Brandeis, 195.
67   *two of the stoutest pillars* Whitman, 1208.
67   *"inviolate personality"* Warren and Brandeis, 205.
67   *"wounded gentility"* Harry Kalven, Jr., quoted in Allen and Mack, 441.
69   *Thomas Cooley* In his *Treatise on the Law of Torts* (1880). Danielson, "The Gender of Privacy and the Embodied Self," 340.
69   *Recent judges* Gerety, "Right of Privacy (update)," 2246.
69   *One scholar contends* Whitman, 1213.
69   *"It is not the breaking"* Solove, "A Brief History of Information Privacy Law," 1–9.
69   *Alvira Roberts* Danielson, "The Gender of Privacy and the Embodied Self," gives a detailed account of the trial and the circumstances leading up to it.
72   *"Alvira Roberts won"* Danielson, 313.
72   *"a vindication of women's modesty"* Allen and Mack, 454.
73   *"the cipher in the case"* Danielson, 322.

10. THE PRIVACY OF THE POOR

74   *Howard Hughes* Didion, "7000 Romaine, Los Angeles 38," *Slouching Towards Bethlehem,* 69–70.
74   *empress Theodora* Runciman, *Byzantine Civilization,* 153.
74   *attending physicians* Holt N. Parker, "Women Doctors in Greece, Rome, and the Byzantine Empire," 131–50.

74 *"Privacy . . . asserts power"* McDougall, *Love-Letters and Privacy in Modern China*, 197.

74 *"privacy on their privy"* Montaigne, "On Three Kinds of Social Intercourse," 933.

74 *"Eavesdropping Zenobia"* Trevor, *Death in Summer*, 6.

75 *duties and ceremonies* Runciman, 151.

75 *By late medieval times* Webb, *Privacy and Solitude in the Middle Ages*, 195–96.

75 *GM executive's salary* Judt, *Ill Fares the Land*, 14.

75 *one in six Americans* Fletcher, "Nearly One in Six in Poverty in the U.S."

75 *privacy fences* Fussell, *Class,* 76–77.

76 *"Time for education"* Marx, *Capital*, 128.

76 *employed in domestic service* Eagleton, *Why Marx Was Right,* 169.

76 *the Reagan administration* Frederick S. Lane, *American Privacy*, 215–16.

77 *"growing 'privacy divide'"* Frederick S. Lane, 219.

77 *the grain of democratic sentiment* Westin, *Privacy and Freedom*, 28.

78 *"economic factors"* Westin, 41.

78 *Egyptian clinics* Inhorn, "Privacy, Privatization, and the Politics of Patronage," 2107.

78 *low-income apartments* Saraceno, "The Italian Family," 477.

78 *the slave* Owens, *This Species of Property*, 136–38. See also Harriet Jacobs, *Incidents in the Life of a Slave Girl: Written by Herself* (1881).

78 *Ota Benga* Cacioppo and Patrick, *Loneliness,* 143–44.

78 *Milan Kundera* Quoted in Jagodzinski, *Privacy and Print*, 93.

79 *"correctional supervision"* Gopnik, "The Caging of America," 73.

79 *against false imprisonment* Karst, "The Freedom of Intimate Association," 631.

79 *Bell v. Wolfish* Karst, "Right of Privacy," 2244. See also Johnson, "Crying *Wolfish*," which discusses *Florence v. Board of Chosen Freeholders* (2012), a case involving blanket strip-search policies.

79 *"dark side of patriarchy"* Levit, "Male Prisoners," 99.

79 *"female guards can view"* Levit, 95–97.

80   *Muslim prisoners* Dannin, *Black Pilgrimage to Islam*, 175–77.

80   *"total institutions"* Lidz, *The Erosion of Autonomy in Long-Term Care*, 142.

80   *Nursing homes* Lidz, 140–51.

81   *"Liberty protects the person"* Quoted in Greene, "Beyond Lawrence," 1869.

82   *"zone of privacy"* Quoted in Warren, "Pride, Shame, and Stigma in Private Spaces," 425.

82   *"The dwelling full of light"* Fromm, *Marx's Concept of Man*, 142.

82   *sleeping under a bridge abutment* "The deprivation we call 'homelessness' concerns not only the dangers of death and illness that prolonged exposure to the elements brings, but also being stripped of a sense of self by not having a space for daily routine and to keep and enjoy certain meaningful things of one's life." Young, *On Female Body Experience,* 159.

82   *"people only have limited"* Solove, "A Brief History of Information Privacy Law," 1–32.

83   *an American CEO* Schor, *The Overworked American*, 19.

83   *English peasant* Schor, 44–51.

83   *domestic chores* Schor, 83–105. For an update showing Schor's 1992 figures to have held true for another decade at least, see "Why Women Are Still Left Doing Most of the Housework."

11. PRIVACY IS NOT PRIVATIZATION

85   *"After a while you learn"* Dylan, *Chronicles, Volume One*, 117–18.

85   *Gerald Ford* Frederick S. Lane, *American Privacy*, 190–91.

85   *a Republican congressman* Huelskamp, "Obamacare HHS Rule Would Give Government Everybody's Health Records." Obviously, I am not in sympathy with Representative Huelskamp's remark. At the same time, honesty compels me to note that in my home state of Vermont, a Democratic administration that has made single-payer health insurance a cornerstone of its political agenda has *also* recommended that police be able to access drug prescription data banks without a search warrant. The latter initiative has been opposed by the state chapter of the ACLU.

85   *an obstacle to better government* Allen, "Privacy in Ameri-

can Law," 30–36. Allen gives a good summary of critiques of privacy from several political viewpoints.

86   *the Swedish model* Orfali, "The Rise and Fall of the Swedish Model," 418–49.

86   *"boomerang kids"* Newman, *The Accordion Family,* 40–41.

87   *the country's Social Democrats* Klinenberg, *Going Solo,* 218.

87   *one of the highest birthrates* Newman, 242.

87   *Maoist phase* Glover, *Humanity,* 296.

88   *Joseph Stalin* Glover, 311.

88   *promoted . . . World Bank* Inhorn, "Privacy, Privatization, and the Politics of Patronage," 2096.

88   *Czech Communist agents* Kriseová, *Václav Havel,* 155.

88   *"Private property . . . stupid"* Fromm, *Marx's Concept of Man,* 132.

89   *"the tendency of all economies"* Everett, "The Social Life of Genes," 54.

89   *human . . . genetic material* Everett, 53–65.

89   *new frontier* I mean "new" relatively speaking. See paragraph below and Skloot, *The Immortal Life of Henrietta Lacks.*

89   *A 2001 survey* Everett, 55.

91   *the property clause* The Oregon Legislature deleted the provision in 2001.

92   *"the world we see groaning"* Eagleton, *Reason, Faith, and Revolution,* 123.

92   *"mistrustfulness increased"* Judt, *Ill Fares the Land,* 15–16.

92   *Privacy Act of 1974* Solove, "A Brief History of Information Privacy Law," 1-26, 1-27.

93   *"fetishistic property protection"* Greene, "Beyond *Lawrence,*" 1889.

93   *Mr. Cooper* Liptak, "Question for Justices."

93   *Olmstead v. United States* Quoted in Whitman, "The Two Western Cultures of Privacy," 1213.

93   *Gary Becker . . . Staffan Linder* Schor, *The Overworked American,* 23.

94   *plan put forward by Raymond Williams* In his book *Communication.*

94   *2011 hacking scandal* See Anthony Lane, "Hack Work."

95   *In 2008 two government employees* American Civil Liberties Union, "America's Surveillance Society."

95   *a bourgeois value* "Private, that is in its positive senses, is a record of the legitimization of a bourgeois view of life." Williams, *Keywords*, 243.

95   *"In a prosperous country"* Orwell, "Not Counting Niggers," 394.

96   *death of Jenny Marx* Fromm, 241.

12. WOMEN AND MEN

97   *"This right of privacy"* Catherine A. MacKinnon, "Privacy v. Equality," 102.

97   *"an odd paradox"* Janna Malamud Smith, *Private Matters*, 206.

97   *Pericles* Thucydides, *The Peloponnesian War*, 109.

98   *historical alignment of female* Rössler, "Gender and Privacy," 53.

98   *for the ancient Greco-Roman world* Arendt, *The Human Condition*, 31–32.

98   *Kate Millett* Allen, *Uneasy Access*, 63.

98   *"It is a sword"* Friedman, *Guarding Life's Dark Secrets*, 233.

98   *not until 1991* Friedman, 234.

98   *Clarence Thomas's claims* Rössler, *The Value of Privacy*, 41.

98   *"had to explode the private"* Catherine A. MacKinnon, 100.

99   *In a 1978 "interview"* Dworkin, *Letters from a War Zone*, 60.

100   *"The conversation of the modest"* Le Guin, "The Conversation of the Modest," 82.

100   *"the womanly virtues"* Le Guin, 78.

101   *"The crux of the matter"* Rössler, *The Value of Privacy*, 36–37.

101   *women on the Oregon Trail* Schlissel, *Women's Diaries of the Westward Journey*, 98–99.

102   *Abigail Adams* McCullough, *John Adams*, 294–95.

103   *"in excess"* Danielson, "The Gender of Privacy and the Embodied Self," 337.

103   *Crystal Eastman* Danielson, 337.

104   *"virtually hostages"* Historian Barbara Weltzer quoted by Allen, *Uneasy Access*, 65.

104   *Female Reform Society* Lasch, *Women and the Common Life*, 79–80.

104   *a tactical shift* Lasch, 87–89.

104   *Elizabeth Cady Stanton* Lasch, 82.

13. WRITERS

106 *"I have a morbid passion"* Anesko, *Letters, Fictions, Lives,* 291–92.

106 *"woman must have money"* Woolf, *A Room of One's Own,* 4.

106 *Harriet Beecher Stowe* Janna Malamud Smith, *Private Matters,* 220.

107 *Alfred Kazin* Mendelson, "The Hidden Life of Alfred Kazin," 52.

107 *"Society for the Protection"* Naomi Black, *Virginia Woolf as Feminist,* 107.

107 *Edmund Wilson* "Celebrity," 114.

107 *Flannery O'Connor* Gooch, *Flannery,* 152.

108 *"There is a marvelous peace"* Fosburgh, "J. D. Salinger Speaks About His Silence."

108 *"a pleasing fancy"* Montaigne, "On Vanity," 1109.

109 *an itch for "reputation . . ."* Montaigne, "On Not Sharing One's Fame," 285.

109 *installing public clocks* Schor, *The Overworked American,* 49.

109 *the work of the artist* Eagleton, *Why Marx Was Right,* 123.

110 *"Writers are always"* Didion, "A Preface," xiv.

110 *Henry James . . . female companions* Coulson *Henry James, Women and Realism.*

110 *Fitzgerald's privately confessed* Hemingway, *A Moveable Feast,* 188–89.

110 *Elizabeth Hardwick's letters* Hamilton, *Robert Lowell,* 418–35.

112 *"family life is private"* Rodriguez, *Hunger of Memory,* 175.

112 *O'Connor was devastated* Gooch, 320.

113 *Nabokov* Brian Boyd, *Vladimir Nabokov,* 611.

113 *William Faulkner* Blotner, *Selected Letters of William Faulkner,* 285.

14. LETTERS

115 *"Everybody reveals"* Adams, "Disciplining the Hand, Disciplining the Heart," 63.

115 *a human presence* Adams, 63. See also Lystra, *Searching the Heart,* 23, and Jagodzinski, *Privacy and Print,* 73–74.

115 *Seneca* Adams, 63.

115   Horace Walpole McDougall, *Love-Letters and Privacy in Modern China*, 183.

115   Thomas Jefferson McCullough, *John Adams*, 145.

116   A number of genre paintings Adams, 63.

116   "a part of my being" Lystra, 12.

116   "more then [sic] kisses" Jagodzinski, 89.

116   "Sir Henry Wotton" Jagodzinski, 88.

116   the "closet" chamber Matthew 6:6.

116   "I cannot bear to open them" Lystra, 22.

116   "as if thy head" Lystra, 23.

117   "The body characterizes" Berry, "Feminism, the Body, and the Machine," 194.

117   "Pray write often" Lystra, 24.

117   "to remember the ladies" McCullough, 104.

117   danger of interception Adams, 64.

117   letters of King Charles I Jagodzinski, 78–86.

118   1710 Post Office Act Frederick S. Lane, *American Privacy*, 7.

118   Alexander Hamilton Frederick S. Lane, 6.

118   In 1792 . . . in 1825 Westin, *Privacy and Freedom*, 335.

119   "To be friends or lovers" Fried, "Privacy," 484.

119   "equivalent of a marriage rite" McDougall, 197.

120   "elevation of the public" McDougall, 193.

120   "men's emotional expression" Lystra, 19–20.

120   Mrs. Eliza Farrar Lystra, 15.

121   Erasmus Adams, 64.

122   "snail paced mails" The journal was *The Friend*.

15. LEFT TO OUR DEVICES

123   "Machinery is adapted" Fromm, *Marx's Concept of Man*, 143.

123   invention of the photograph Frederick S. Lane, *American Privacy*, 21–22.

123   earliest U.S. court cases Allen, "Privacy," 22; Allen and Mack, "How Privacy Got Its Gender," 459, 461–62.

123   Samuel B. Morse Frederick S. Lane, 23–27.

124   the 4S Halpern, "Over the High-Tech Rainbow," 37.

124   "Putting aside the issue" Halpern, "Over the High-Tech Rainbow," 37.

125   *Sony, Citibank* Fallows, "Hacked," 106.

125   *WikiLeaks* Caryl, "Why WikiLeaks Changes Everything," 27.

125   *Ron Ritchey* Fallows, 113.

125   *"If you put the fates"* Berry, "Word and Flesh," *What Are People For?*, 203.

125   *"Singularity"* Halpern, "Over the High-Tech Rainbow," 37.

126   *"seamlessly part of us"* Chorost, *World Wide Mind*, 10.

126   *story of Apple Computer* Frederick S. Lane, 198–204.

126   *500 million active users* "Celebrity," 157.

126   *private fortunes* Alterman, "Steve Jobs," 9.

126   *a man whose castle* According to the *London Daily Mail* (March 4, 2009), the family of Bill and Melinda Gates "live in a vast mansion on the shores of Lake Washington and are very protective of the privacy of their children."

126   *"What increasingly emerges"* Žižek, *Violence*, 41.

127   *Video Privacy Protection Act* Solove, "A Brief History of Information Privacy Law," 1–34.

127   *"entire life . . . open book"* Frederick S. Lane, 259.

128   *Carrier IQ* Lutz, "Carrier IQ."

128   *United States v. Jones* Jeffrey Rosen, "Interpreting the Constitution in the Digital Era."

128   *cloud-connected cars* Halpern, "Over the High-Tech Rainbow," 37.

130   *Chinese assemblers* Alterman and Kennedy, *The Right to Privacy*, 9.

131   *net neutrality* Wu, *The Master Switch*, 287ff.

131   *"IBM is worse"* Havel, *Disturbing the Peace*, 14.

131   *roughly a quarter* Pew Research Center, "Who's Online?" See also Fairlee, *Are We Really a Nation Online?*

16. STORIES THAT BEGIN IN AIRPORTS

133   *"None of us know"* Havel, *Disturbing the Peace*, 109.

133   *typical American home* Klinenberg, *Going Solo*, 48–49.

134   *"Those who . . . live off the grid"* Nick Rosen, *Off the Grid*, 219.

134   *communes* McLaughlin and Davidson, *Builders of the Dawn*, 67; Timothy Miller, *The 60s Communes*, 193–95, 227.

134   *kibbutzim* Gavron, *The Kibbutz*, 1; Westin, *Privacy and Freedom*, 59.

135   *"It was the carbon"* Monbiot, *Heat*, 173.

136   *John Tyner* "The Uproar."

136   *"blob" machine* Jeffrey Rosen, *The Deciders*, 4–6. For an earlier and fuller discussion, including differences in how the U.S. and Europe dealt with the issue, see Jeffrey Rosen's "Nude Breach."

137   *Facebook users outraged* Gannes, "The Apologies of Zuckerberg."

17. BODY AND SOUL

140   *"Yet it seems to me"* Robinson, "Night Thoughts of a Baffled Humanist," 30–31.

140   *"Even the criminal thought"* Fromm, *Marx's Concept of Man*, 82.

141   *torture* Scarry, *The Body in Pain*, 54.

142   *common household objects* Scarry, *The Body in Pain*, 38–45.

142   *"so 1997"* Petri, "iPhone and iPad Track Users' Movement."

143   *"Nothing More Public"* Berlant and Warner, "Sex in Public," 329.

144   *Laura Kipnis* "Up Front," *New York Times Book Review*, July 14, 2011.

144   *"offensive to a reasonable person"* Alderman and Kennedy, *The Right to Privacy*, 156, 187.

144   *"the steady hemorrhage"* Eagleton, *Why Marx Was Right*, xii.

145   *Planned Parenthood v. Casey* Greene, "Beyond *Lawrence*," 1894.

145   *Bruce Mazlish* Slouka, *War of the Worlds*, 68–72.

147   *seventy-seven cents* Fitzpatrick "Why Do Women Still Earn Less Than Men?" The figure drops to sixty-eight cents for African American women and fifty-eight cents for Hispanic women.

18. ANOTHER NATIVITY

149   *"I would not open"* Jagodzinski, *Privacy and Print*, 92.

149   *"pregnant woman"* My ruminations on pregnancy and pri-

vacy were prompted by my first conversation with this book's editor, David Rogers.

150 *"nothing more unsociable"* Montaigne, "On Solitude," 267.

150 *two pregnant women* Both have asked to remain anonymous.

152 *an Inuit man* Best, *A True Discourse of the Late Voyages of Discoverie*, 63.

152 *Four gunmen* Nassau, New York, 1982.

153 *Japanese Americans* Dickerson, *Inside America's Concentration Camps*, 88.

153 *trinket box* Moshenska and Myers, *Archaeologies of Internment*, 133.

BIBLIOGRAPHY

Aboujaoude, Elias. "Violin Requiem for Privacy: The Tyler Clementi Story." PsychologyToday.com, October 13, 2010.

Abu-Lughod, Lila. *Veiled Sentiments: Honor and Poetry in a Bedouin Society.* Berkeley: University of California Press, 1986.

Adams, Ann Jensen. "Disciplining the Hand, Disciplining the Heart: Letter-Writing Paintings and Practices in Seventeenth-Century Holland." In *Love Letters: Dutch Genre Painting in the Age of Vermeer.* Ed. Peter Sutton et al. London: Frances Lincoln Limited, 2003.

Alderman, Ellen, and Caroline Kennedy. *The Right to Privacy.* New York: Alfred A. Knopf, 1995.

Allen, Anita L. *Uneasy Access: Privacy for Women in a Free Society.* Totowa, NJ: Rowman & Littlefield, 1988.

———. "Privacy in American Law." In Rössler, *Privacies.*

Allen, Anita L., and Erin Mack. "How Privacy Got Its Gender." *Northern Illinois University Law Review* 10 (1989–1990): 441–78.

Alterman, Eric. "Steve Jobs: An American 'Disgrace.'" *The Nation,* November 28, 2011.

Altman, Irwin. "Privacy Regulation: Culturally Universal or Culturally Specific?" *Journal of Social Ideas* 33, no. 3 (1977): 66–84.

American Civil Liberties Union. *America's Surveillance Society.* ACLU.org, 2011.

Amichai, Yehuda. *Selected Poetry.* Trans. Chana Bloch and Stephen Mitchell. Berkeley: University of California Press, 1996.

Anesko, Michael. *Letters, Fictions, Lives: Henry James and William Dean Howells.* New York: Oxford University Press, 1997.

Arendt, Hannah. *The Human Condition.* Chicago: University of Chicago Press, 1958.

Associated Press. "U.S. Official: Privacy Must Be Redefined." MSNBC.com, November 11, 2007.

Auden, W. H. *The Dyer's Hand and Other Essays.* New York: Vintage, 1968.

Banks, Russell. *Dreaming Up America*. New York: Seven Stories Press, 2008.

Berlant, Lauren, and Michael Warner. "Sex in Public." In *Intimacy*. Ed. Lauren Berlant. Chicago: University of Chicago Press, 2000.

Berry, Wendell. *What Are People For?* New York: North Point Press, 1990.

Best, George. *A True Discourse of the Late Voyages of Discoverie, for the Finding of a Passage to Cathaia* (1578). In *Tokens of Possession: The Voyages of Martin Frobisher*. Ed. Walter A. Kenyon. Toronto: Royal Ontario Museum, 1975.

Black, Donald. *Moral Time*. New York: Oxford University Press, 2011.

Black, Naomi. *Virginia Woolf as Feminist*. Ithaca: Cornell University Press, 2004.

Blotner, Joseph. *Selected Letters of William Faulkner*. New York: Vintage, 1978.

Bonhoeffer, Dietrich. *Life Together*. Trans. John W. Doberstein. London: SCM Press, 1954.

Boswell, James. *Life of Samuel Johnson, L.L.D.* Great Books of the Western World 44. Chicago: Encyclopedia Britannica, 1952.

Boyd, Brian. *Vladimir Nabokov: The American Years*. Princeton: Princeton University Press, 2004.

Boyd, Nan Alamilla. *Wide Open Town: A History of Queer San Francisco to 1965*. Berkeley: University of California Press, 2003.

Bulfinch, Thomas. *The Age of Fable*. 1855; New York: Harper and Row, 1966.

Cacioppo, John T., and William Patrick. *Loneliness: Human Nature and the Need for Social Connection*. New York: Norton, 2008.

Caryl, Christian. "Why WikiLeaks Changes Everything." *New York Review of Books,* January 13, 2011.

"Celebrity." *Lapham's Quarterly* 4, no. 1 (Winter 2011).

Chaucer, Geoffrey. "The Miller's Tale." In *The Works of Geoffrey Chaucer*, 2nd ed. Ed. F. N. Robinson. Boston: Houghton Mifflin, 1957.

Chorost, Michael. *World Wide Mind: The Coming Integration of Humanity, Machines, and the Internet*. New York: Simon & Schuster, 2011.

Cole, David. "Privacy 2.0." *Nation,* December 5, 2011.

Coulson, Victoria. *Henry James, Women and Realism*. Cambridge: Cambridge University Press, 2007.

Danielson, Caroline. "The Gender of Privacy and the Embodied Self: Examining the Origins of the Right to Privacy in U.S. Law." *Feminist Studies* 25, no. 2 (Summer 1999): 311–44.

Dannin, Robert. *Black Pilgrimage to Islam*. New York: Oxford University Press, 2002.

Dickerson, James L. *Inside America's Concentration Camps: Two Centuries of Internment and Torture*. Chicago: Chicago Review Press, 2010.

Didion, Joan. *Slouching Towards Bethlehem*. New York: Farrar, Straus and Giroux, 1968.

Doyle, Charles. *The USA Patriot Act: A Legal Analysis*. Congressional Research Service, Library of Congress, April 15, 2002. Order Code RL31377.

Dworkin, Andrea. *Letters from a War Zone: Writings 1976–1989*. New York: Dutton, 1989.

Dylan, Bob. *Chronicles, Volume One*. New York: Simon & Schuster, 1994.

Eagleton, Terry. *Reason, Faith, and Revolution: Reflections on the God Debate*. New Haven: Yale University Press, 2009.

———. *Why Marx Was Right*. New Haven: Yale University Press, 2011.

Edwards, Douglas. *I'm Feeling Lucky: The Confessions of Google Employee Number 59*. New York: Houghton Mifflin Harcourt, 2011.

Eliot, T. S. "Burnt Norton." In *Four Quartets*. New York: Harcourt, Brace & World, 1971.

Everett, Margaret. "The Social Life of Genes: Privacy, Property and the New Genetics." *Social Science & Medicine* 56 (2003): 53–65.

Fairlee, Robert W. *Are We Really a Nation Online? Ethnic and Racial Disparities in Access to Technology and Their Consequences*. Report for the Leadership Conference on Civil Rights Education, September 20, 2005.

Fallows, James. "Hacked." *Atlantic Monthly*, November 2011.

Fielder, Christine, and Chris King. *Sexual Paradox: Complementarity, Reproductive Conflict and Human Emergence*. Kila, MT: Whitefish, Kessinger Publishing, 2006.

Fitzpatrick, Laura. "Why Do Women Still Earn Less Than Men?" *Time*, April 20, 2010.

Fletcher, Michael A. "Nearly One in Six in Poverty in the U.S.; Children Hit Hard, Census Says." *Washington Post*, September 13, 2011.

Foderaro, Lisa W. "Private Moment Made Public, Then a Fatal Jump." NewYorkTimes.com, September 29, 2010.

Fosburgh, Lacey. "J. D. Salinger Speaks About His Silence." *New York Times*, November 3, 1974.

Fried, Charles. "Privacy." *Yale Law Journal* 77, no. 3 (January 1968): 475–93.

Friedman, Lawrence M. *Guarding Life's Dark Secrets: Legal and Social Controls over Reputation, Property, and Privacy.* Stanford: Stanford University Press, 2007.

Fromm, Erich. *Marx's Concept of Man.* With a translation of Marx's Economic and Philosophical Manuscripts by J. B. Bottomore. New York: Frederick Ungar, 1961.

Fussell, Paul. *Class: A Guide Through the American Status System.* New York: Touchstone, 1992.

Gannes, Liz. "The Apologies of Zuckerberg: A Retrospective." AllThingsDigital.com, November 29, 2011.

Gavron, Daniel. *The Kibbutz: Awakening from Utopia.* New York: Rowman & Littlefield, 2000.

Gerety, Tom. "Right of Privacy." In Levy and Karst, *Encyclopedia of the American Constitution.*

Ghosh, Oroon. *The Dance of Shiva and Other Tales from India.* New York: New American Library, 1965.

Gifford, Jonathan. Interview with Christian Heller. *Spark* (CBC), June 18, 2011.

Gleick, James. "How Google Dominates Us." *New York Review of Books,* August 18, 2011.

Glover, Jonathan. *Humanity: A Moral History of the Twentieth Century.* New Haven: Yale University Press, 2000.

Gooch, Brad. *Flannery: A Life of Flannery O'Connor.* New York: Little, Brown, 2009.

Gopnik, Adam. "The Caging of America: Why Do We Lock Up So Many People?" *New Yorker,* January 30, 2012.

Greene, Jamal. "Beyond *Lawrence*: Metaprivacy and Punishment." *Yale Law Journal* 115 (2006): 1862–1928.

Hallie, Philip P. *Lest Innocent Blood Be Shed: The Story of the Village of Le Chambon and How Goodness Happened There.* 1979; New York: HarperCollins, 1994.

Halpern, Sue. "Mind Control and the Internet." *New York Review of Books*, June 23, 2011.

———. "Over the High-Tech Rainbow." *New York Review of Books*, November 24, 2011.

Hamilton, Ian. *Robert Lowell: A Biography.* New York: Random House, 1982.

Havel, Václav. *Disturbing the Peace: A Conversation with Karel Hvíždala.* New York: Alfred A. Knopf, 1990.

Heffernan, Virginia. "Too Much Vérité." NewYorkTimes.com, April 17, 2011.

Helft, Miguel, and Claire Cain Miller. "1986 Privacy Law Is Outrun by the Web." *New York Times*, January 9, 2011.

Hemingway, Ernest. *A Moveable Feast.* 1964; New York: Signet, 1967.

Huelskamp, Tim. "Obamacare HHS Rule Would Give Government Everybody's Health Records." *Washington Examiner*, September 23, 2011.

Inhorn, Marcia C. "Privacy, Privatization, and the Politics of Patronage: Ethnographic Challenges to Penetrating the Secret World of Middle Eastern, Hospital-Based In Vitro Fertilization." *Social Science & Medicine* 59 (2004): 2095–108.

Inness, Julie C. *Privacy, Intimacy, and Isolation.* New York: Oxford University Press, 1992.

"The iPhone: Tracking Where You've Been." *The Week*, May 6, 2011.

Jagodzinski, Cecile M. *Privacy and Print: Reading and Writing in Seventeenth-Century England.* Charlottesville: University Press of Virginia, 1999.

Jeffers, Robinson. *Cawdor and Medea.* New York: New Directions, 1970.

Johnson, Aaron. "Crying *Wolfish*: The Upcoming Challenge to Blanket Strip-Search Policies in *Florence v. Board of Chosen Freeholders.*" *Duke Law Review* 7 (2011): 41–59.

Judt, Tony. *Ill Fares the Land.* New York: Penguin, 2010.

Julian of Norwich. *Revelations of Divine Love.* Trans. Elizabeth Spearing. New York: Penguin, 1998.

Karst, Kenneth L. "The Freedom of Intimate Association." *Yale Law Journal* 89, no. 4 (March 1980): 624–92.

———. "Right of Privacy." In Levy and Karst, *Encyclopedia of the American Constitution*.

Keizer, Garret. "Requiem for the Private Word." *Harper's Magazine*, August 2008.

Kelly, Anita. *The Psychology of Secrets*. New York: Kluwer Academic/Plenum, 2002.

Kirn, Walter. "Little Brother Is Watching." *New York Times Magazine*, October 15, 2010.

Klinenberg, Eric. *Going Solo: The Extraordinary Rise and Surprising Appeal of Living Alone*. New York: Penguin, 2012.

Koestenbaum, Wayne. *Humiliation*. New York: Picador, 2011.

Kriseová, Eda. *Václav Havel: The Authorized Biography*. Trans. Caleb Crain. New York: St. Martin's Press, 1993.

Lamb, Charles. *Essays of Elia*. 1823; New York: A. L. Burt, 1885.

Lane, Anthony. "Hack Work: A Tabloid Culture Runs Amok." *New Yorker*, August 1, 2011.

Lane, Frederick S. *American Privacy: The 400-Year History of Our Most Contested Right*. Boston: Beacon Press, 2009.

Lasch, Christopher. *Women and the Common Life: Love, Marriage, and Feminism*. Ed. Elizabeth Lasch-Quinn. New York: Norton, 1997.

Le Guin, Ursula K. "The Conversation of the Modest." In *The Wild Girls Plus . . .* Oakland, CA: PM Press, 2011.

Levit, Nancy. "Male Prisoners: Privacy, Suffering, and the Legal Construction of Masculinity." In *Prison Masculinities*. Ed. Don Sabo, Terry A. Kupers, and Willie London. Philadelphia: Temple University Press, 2001.

Levy, Leonard W., and Kenneth L. Karst, eds. *Encyclopedia of the American Constitution*, 2nd ed. New York: Macmillan, 2000.

Lidz, Charles W., Lynn Fischer, and Robert M. Arnold. *The Erosion of Autonomy in Long-Term Care*. New York: Oxford University Press, 1992.

Liptak, Adam. "Justices Say GPS Tracker Violated Privacy Rights." *New York Times*, January 23, 2012.

———. "Question for Justices: If Privacy Is Violated, When Is the Government Liable?" *New York Times*, November 30, 2011.

Lutz, Zachary. "Carrier IQ: What It Is, What It Isn't, and What You Need to Know." EndGadget.com, December 1, 2011.

Lystra, Karen. *Searching the Heart: Women, Men, and Romantic Love in Nineteenth-Century America.* New York: Oxford University Press, 1989.

MacKinnon, Catherine A. "Privacy v. Equality: Beyond Roe v. Wade." In *Feminism Unmodified: Discourses on Life and Law.* Cambridge, MA: Harvard University Press, 1987.

MacKinnon, Rebecca. "Shi Tao, Yahoo!, and the Lessons for Corporate and Social Responsibility." Rconversation.blogs.com, December 30, 2007.

"Mao Thinks Well of Nixon." *Evening Independent,* July 9, 1975.

Martin, John P. "Lower Merion District's Laptop Saga Ends with $610,000 Settlement." *Philadelphia Inquirer,* October 12, 2010.

Marx, Karl. *Capital.* Ed. Friedrich Engels. Great Books of the Western World 50. Chicago: Encyclopedia Britannica, 1952.

McCullough, David. *John Adams.* New York: Simon & Schuster, 2001.

McDougall, Bonnie S. *Love-Letters and Privacy in Modern China: The Intimate Lives of Lu Xun and Xu Guangping.* Oxford: Oxford University Press, 2002.

McLaughlin, Corinne, and Gordon Davidson. *Builders of the Dawn: Community Lifestyles in a Changing World.* Summertown, TN: Book Publishing Company, 1985.

Mendelson, Edward. "The Hidden Life of Alfred Kazin." *New York Review of Books,* August 18, 2011.

Miller, James. *The Passion of Michel Foucault.* New York: Simon & Schuster, 1993.

Miller, Timothy. *The 60s Communes: Hippies and Beyond.* Syracuse: Syracuse University Press, 1999.

Monbiot, George. *Heat: How to Stop the Planet from Burning.* Cambridge, MA: South End Press, 2009.

Montaigne, Michel de. *The Complete Essays.* Trans. M. A. Screech. London: Penguin, 2003.

Moore, Jr., Barrington. *Privacy: Studies in Social and Cultural History.* Armonk, NY, and London: M. E. Sharpe, 1984.

Moshenska, Gabriel, and Adrian Myers, eds. *Archaeologies of Internment.* New York: Springer, 2011.

Newman, Katherine. *The Accordion Family: Boomerang Kids, Anxious Parents, and the Private Toll of Global Competition*. Boston: Beacon, 2012.

Nimmer, Melville B. "Privacy and the First Amendment." In Levy and Karst, *Encyclopedia of the American Constitution*.

Nippert-Eng, Christena. *Islands of Privacy*. Chicago: University of Chicago Press, 2010.

Orfali, Kristina. "The Rise and Fall of the Swedish Model." In Prost and Vincent, *Riddles of Identity in Modern Times*.

Orwell, George. "Not Counting Niggers" (1939). In *An Age Like This 1920–1940*, Vol. 1, *The Collected Essays, Journalism and Letters*. Ed. Sonia Orwell and Ian Angus. New York: Harcourt Brace Jovanovich, 1968.

Owens, Leslie Howard. *This Species of Property: Slave Life and Culture in the Old South*. New York: Oxford University Press, 1976.

Paine, Thomas. *Common Sense & The Rights of Man*. Ed. Tony Benn. London: Phoenix Press, 2000.

Parker, Holt N. "Women Doctors in Greece. Rome, and the Byzantine Empire." In *Women Physicians and Healers: Climbing a Long Hill*. Ed. Lilian R. Furst. Lexington: University Press of Kentucky, 1997.

Parker, Ian. "The Story of a Suicide: Two College Roommates, a Webcam, and a Tragedy." *New Yorker*, February 6, 2012.

Petersen, Charles. "Google and Money." *New York Review of Books*, December 9, 2010.

Petri, Alexandra. "iPhone and iPad Track Users' Movement. Do We Care?" *Washington Post*, April 20, 2011.

Pew Research Center. "Who's Online: Internet User Demographics." Pew Research Center's Internet and American Life Project, 2010–2011.

Plath, Sylvia. "Insomniac." In *Eight American Poets*. Ed. Joel Conarroe. New York: Vintage, 1997.

Priest, Dana, and William M. Arkin. "A Hidden World, Growing Beyond Control." *Washington Post*, July 19, 2010.

Prost, Antoine, and Gérard Vincent, eds. *Riddles of Identity in Modern Times*, Vol. 5, *A History of Private Life*. Trans. Arthur Goldhammer. Cambridge, MA: Belknap Press of Harvard University, 1991.

Rafay, Atif. "On the Margins of Freedom." WalrusMagazine.com. April 2011.

Robinson, Marilynne. "Night Thoughts of a Baffled Humanist." *Nation,* November 28, 2011.

Rodriguez, Richard. *Hunger of Memory: The Education of Richard Rodriguez.* New York: Bantam, 1983.

Rosen, Jeffrey. *The Deciders: Facebook, Google, and the Future of Privacy and Free Speech.* Governance Studies at Brookings, May 2, 2011.

———. "Interpreting the Constitution in the Digital Era." Interview with Terry Gross. *Fresh Air,* NPR, November 30, 2011.

———. "Nude Breach: Why Privacy Always Loses." *New Republic,* December 12, 2010.

Rosen, Nick. *Off the Grid: Inside the Movement for More Space, Less Government, and True Independence in Modern America.* New York: Penguin, 2010.

Rössler, Beate. "Gender and Privacy: A Critique of the Liberal Tradition." In Rössler, *Privacies.*

———, ed. *Privacies: Philosophical Evaluations.* Stanford: Stanford University Press, 2004.

———. *The Value of Privacy.* Trans. R. D. V. Glasgow. Cambridge, UK: Polity, 2005.

Roth, Philip. *The Human Stain.* New York: Random House, 2000.

Runciman, Steven. *Byzantine Civilization.* 1933; New York: Meridian, 1956.

Saltz, Gail. *Anatomy of a Secret Life: The Psychology of Living a Lie.* New York: Morgan Road Books, 2006.

Samar, Vincent J. *The Right to Privacy: Gays, Lesbians, and the Constitution.* Philadelphia: Temple University Press, 1992.

Saraceno, Chiara. "The Italian Family: Paradoxes of Privacy." In Prost and Vincent, *Riddles of Identity in Modern Times.*

Scarry, Elaine. *The Body in Pain: The Making and Unmaking of the World.* New York: Oxford University Press, 1985.

———. *Rule of Law, Misrule of Men.* Cambridge: MIT (a *Boston Review* book), 2010.

Schlissel, Lillian. *Women's Diaries of the Westward Journey.* New York: Schocken, 1982.

Schor, Juliet B. *The Overworked American: The Unexpected Decline of Leisure.* New York: Basic Books, 1992.

Schumpeter, Joseph. *Capitalism, Socialism and Democracy.* London: Routledge, 1994.

Sedgwick, Eve Kosofsky. *Epistemology of the Closet.* Berkeley: University of California Press, 1990.

Shklar, Judith N. *Ordinary Vices.* Cambridge, MA: Belknap Press of Harvard University, 1984.

Shostak, Marjorie. *Nisa: The Life and Words of a !Kung Woman.* Cambridge, MA: Harvard University Press, 1981.

Singer, Peter. "Visible Man: Ethics in a World Without Secrets." *Harper's Magazine,* August 2011.

Skloot, Rebecca. *The Immortal Life of Henrietta Lacks.* New York: Crown, 2010.

Slouka, Mark. *War of the Worlds: Cyberspace and the High-Tech Assault on Reality.* New York: Basic Books, 1995.

Smith, Janna Malamud. *Private Matters: In Defense of the Personal Life.* Reading, MA: Addison-Wesley, 1997.

Solove, Daniel J. "A Brief History of Information Privacy Law." In *Proskauer on Privacy.* Ed. Christopher Wolf. New York: Practicing Law Institute, 2006.

———. *Understanding Privacy.* Cambridge, MA: Harvard University Press, 2008.

Storr, Anthony. *Solitude: A Return to the Self.* New York: The Free Press, 1988.

Thomas, Elizabeth Marshall. *The Harmless People.* New York: Alfred A. Knopf, 1959.

Thomson, Judith Jarvis. "The Right to Privacy." *Philosophy and Public Affairs* 4, no. 4 (Summer 1975): 295–314.

Thucydides. *The Peloponnesian War.* Trans. John H. Finley, Jr. New York: Modern Library, 1951.

Tocqueville, Alexis de. *Democracy in America.* 1835; New York: Vintage, 1945.

Trevor, William. *Death in Summer.* New York: Viking, 1998.

Trotsky, Leon. *My Life.* New York: Pathfinder Press, 1970.

"The Uproar Over Body Scanners and Pat-Downs," *The Week,* December 3, 2010.

van Manen, Max, and Bas Levering. *Childhood's Secrets: Intimacy, Privacy, and the Self Reconsidered.* New York: Teachers College Press, 1996.

Warren, Carol A. B. "Pride, Shame, and Stigma to Private Spaces." *Ethnography* 11, no. 3 (2010): 425–42.

Warren, Samuel D., and Louis D. Brandeis. "The Right to Privacy." *Harvard Law Review* 4, no. 5 (December 15, 1890).

Webb, Diana. *Privacy and Solitude in the Middle Ages.* New York: Hambledon Continuum, 2007.

Westin, Alan W. *Privacy and Freedom.* New York: Atheneum, 1967.

Whitman, James Q. "The Two Western Cultures of Privacy: Dignity Versus Liberty." *Yale Law Journal* 113 (2004): 1153–221.

"Why Women Are Still Left Doing Most of the Housework." University of Oxford, May 23, 2011. http://www.ox.ac.uk/media/news_stories/2011/112304_1.html.

Williams, Raymond. *Communication.* Harmondsworth, UK: Penguin, 1962.

———. "Private." In *Keywords: A Vocabulary of Culture and Society,* Rev. ed. New York: Oxford University Press, 1985.

Woolf, Virginia. *A Room of One's Own.* 1929; New York: Harcourt, 2005.

Wu, Tim. *The Master Switch: The Rise and Fall of Information Empires.* New York: Alfred A. Knopf, 2011.

Young, Iris Marion. *On Female Body Experience: "Throwing Like a Girl" and Other Essays.* New York: Oxford University Press, 2005.

Žižek, Slavoj. *Violence: Six Sideways Reflections.* New York: Picador, 2008.

ACKNOWLEDGMENTS

Heartfelt thanks to David Rogers, my editor; to Frances Coady, our supporter at Picador; to Jim Rutman and Peter Matson, my agents; and to Simone Rowen, my research assistant. Absent any one of them, this book might never have appeared.

For their care and attention at various stages of the book's production, Kolt Beringer, Elizabeth Bruce, and Henry Kaufman also have my thanks.

I am grateful to Clara Jeffery of *Mother Jones* and Ellen Rosenbush of *Harper's Magazine*, who encouraged my first attempts at writing about privacy.

Thanks, yet again, to Kim Crady-Smith of Green Mountain Books and to the librarians of Lyndon State College, the University of Vermont, and Dartmouth-Hitchcock Medical Center, especially Jay Bona, Garet Nelson, June Trayah, and Cheryl Wheelock, all of whom were invaluable resources, as were those individuals who kindly provided information: Heidi Bohaker, Kira Brunner Don, Elizabeth Galle, Robert Gensberg, Addison Hall, Fred Hiatt, Sarah Keizer, Amy Leal, Ian MacLaren, Ethan Marcotte, Mary Norris, Genevieve Plunkett, Maya Shapiro, Vaska Tumir, Charlotte Wyatt, and David Yaffe.

Thanks, not least of all, to my friend Howard Frank Mosher, who read and commented on this book as it developed, and to my wife, Kathy Keizer, who performed the same office while continuing to teach me the joys of private life.

INDEX